Contents

Page 2: The Olympic flag waves amid national flags at the 128th International Olympic Committee Session in Kuala Lumpur, Malaysia, in 2015, where Beijing was selected as the host city for the 2022 Olympic Winter Games.
Opposite: Runners compete in the 400-meter semifinals at the London Olympic Games in 2012.

FOREWORD | APOLO OHNO

The Olympic family is pretty tight. After all, how many people do you know who can rightly claim to be among the top two or three in their field in the entire country? The path to such a title is difficult, but as Tom Hanks' character said in the movie *A League of Their Own,* "The hard is what makes it great." For those of us who have enjoyed the privilege of standing on a medal podium, the bond is even greater. Olympic and Paralympic medalists are often gathered at fundraisers or premieres, and occasionally we are even asked to dance on television. Most of us are happy to use our athletic success to help others, and so we'll often accept invitations to kick off other worthwhile programs or events. The green room is a great place to make friends or renew acquaintances. It is at such times that we get to exchange our Olympic stories or learn about each other's sports.

The path to [an Olympic] title is difficult, but as Tom Hanks' character said in the movie *A League of Their Own,* "The hard is what makes it great."

John Naber comes to many such events. He always seems to be looking for interesting stories or facts about the Games. I recall meeting him at the USA House in Salt Lake City, where Olympians and their guests could mingle with donors and sponsors at the Games. John drove to Utah from his home in Pasadena, California, just to watch other Olympians compete. I remember his strong handshake and outgoing smile; he was eager to connect with this new generation of Olympians. I had heard that Naber, then president of the USOPA (the U.S. Olympians and Paralympians Association, our alumni, if you will), was the guy to "connect the dots" for each new class of Olympic athletes.

At another time, John and I agreed to escort members of the upcoming International Special Olympics team down a red carpet at a publicity launch inside the Staples Center (the sports arena in Los Angeles). John loves to connect Olympians and their stories. One of John's favorite questions of an Olympian is: "What's the most interesting Olympic trivia question to which your name is the answer?" My question appears in this book, hidden inside another Olympian's story.

When I heard that John was compiling many of his favorite Olympic and Paralympic stories into a book, I quickly agreed to write this foreword because I knew how

At any Olympic gathering—no matter the country, summer theme or winter—there's nothing more familiar and comforting than the sight and sound of John Naber. Not because he's an Olympic legend (he is), and not because he's got such high integrity and character (he does), instead it's because John is a relentless, unabashed, "gold medal" Olympic storyteller and fan. If you ever have the chance, plant yourself next to him. You will walk away with a priceless memory! —Karch Kiraly, the only volleyball player to win Olympic gold in both beach and indoor ■ **With his wonderful sense of humor and curiosity, John is a wealth of knowledge and fun facts. —Greg Louganis,** the most celebrated Olympic diver in history ■ **John Naber has told me things about my own competitive career that even I didn't know! —Shannon Miller,** America's most decorated Olympic gymnast ■ **Whether in the pool, on the ice, rounding the track, balancing on a beam, or scoring the winning point, John's ability to wax poetic about ALL athletes/events will captivate any audience. —Brandi Chastain,** featured on the cover of *Sports Illustrated* after 1999 World Cup win ■ **John... inspires me to learn more and understand our unique position in society through his knowledge and entertainment skills. —Jonny Moseley,** inventor of the "Dinner Roll/Iron Cross" that changed mogul skiing forever ■ **John Naber is a student of the Olympic Games and he knows how to put them in historical context. He loves sharing stories about the individuals who make history. —Tommie Smith,** internationally renowned civil rights advocate ■ **John is an enthusiastic historian and storyteller, which has led him to become an Olympic trivia expert. You will enjoy his new book. John, I salute you! —Peggy Fleming,** America's only gold medalist at the 1968 Olympic Winter Games in Grenoble ■ **You can bet this is a Gold Medal Collection you'll enjoy with your family and friends! —Dick Fosbury,** inventor of the "Fosbury Flop." ■ **John Naber possesses an unprecedented talent as a storyteller and an overflowing treasure chest of captivating stories about Olympians, Paralympians, and the Olympic and Paralympic Games. —Candace Cable,** the first Paralympian to medal in both Winter and Summer Paralympic events ■ **I have been stumped countless times as Naber hosted "Olympic Jeopardy" at various gatherings through the years. Get ready to be entertained! —Dan Jansen,** who carried his daughter around the ice after his long overdue Olympic win ■ **Many people—Olympians, Paralympians, and non-athletes alike—know John Naber for his encyclopedic knowledge of Olympic competition—not just the mainstream, premier events and not just men's sports either. This book gives the broader public an opportunity to meet this master storyteller. You will want to share the love. —Wyomia Tyus,** the first person to successfully defend an Olympic 100-meter dash title ■ **Naber always challenges us with fun, challenging, and sometimes quirky questions. If you are a fan of the Olympics, you will love John's book. —Bart Conner,** the only male gymnast to win gold at every major level of U.S. national and international competition

OLYMPIC TRIVIA CHALLENGE!

100 Questions and the Remarkable Stories Behind Them

JOHN NABER

FOREWORD BY **APOLO OHNO**

3
5
6
7
8
9

America's most decorated Winter Olympian, short track speed skater Apolo Ohno leads as he leans into a turn.

interesting his book was going to be. His questions address many more sports than his own sport of swimming. The stories gathered here cover Summer, Winter, and Paralympic Games, national and international heroes, historical records and recent developments, what happened on the field of play, as well as what Olympians have done after their athletic accomplishments have passed.

This book may not be a reference or research manual, but it certainly will engage the hearts and minds of Olympic and Paralympic fans and hopefuls for decades to come. Enjoy!

– **APOLO OHNO**

Short track speed skating, 2002, 2006, 2010, 4 gold medals, 2 silvers, 4 bronzes, America's most decorated Winter Olympian, USOP Hall of Fame, Champion, Dancing With the Stars *Season 4,* New York Times *best-selling author*

INTRODUCTION | JOHN NABER

When I was 10 years old, my family stopped in Olympia, Greece, on a Mediterranean vacation cruise. The tour guide took us through the tunnel that led to the Stade (origin of the word "stadium") where the athletes in ancient Greece used to compete. The guide told us that anyone caught cheating in the ancient Games would be punished by having a statue carved in his likeness and placed on display in the tunnel for all future competitors to see. The cost of the statue was billed to the athlete's hometown. The mere sight of these statues would make each competitor think twice before contemplating any "shortcuts" of his own.

I was so impressed that the Olympic ideals were so committed to sportsmanship and fair play that I looked up to my parents and said, "Mom, Dad, I think I want to be an Olympian, someday." "Really?" Mom replied, "In what sport?" Neither of us had any idea, because I was not a very good athlete. I would not join my first swim team for another three years, but something about the Olympic movement had tickled my fancy. Ten years later, as a member of the U.S. Olympic swim team, I would compete in the 1976 Olympic Games in Montreal in the backstroke, freestyle, and relay events. Since then I have become, and remain, a devoted fan of the Olympic Games.

Olympic champions are not extraordinary people. We are ordinary people who have found a way to accomplish extraordinary results in the area of life that matters most to us.

After I returned with four gold medals and one silver from the Games in Montreal, someone pointed out that my 200-meter backstroke world record time had surpassed the records in the men's butterfly and the women's freestyle for the first time in history. I may not have surpassed Mark Spitz's seven-gold-medal haul in Munich, but it was a statistic that gave me great pleasure, even if nobody else knew about it. In this way, my love of Olympic trivia was born.

Following my retirement from swimming in 1977, I received various invitations to work as an expert analyst on upcoming television coverage of my sport. When the U.S. team was asked to boycott the 1980 Olympic Games in Moscow, I enjoyed an additional four years as America's most recent Olympic swimming champion,

John Naber (center), winner of four gold medals and a silver at the 1976 Olympic Games in Montreal, joins U.S. teammates on the medal podium.

and during that time I was also invited to cover a variety of other Olympic sports for radio and television. My broadcasting career includes coverage of more than 30 Olympic sports and 10 Olympic Games (both summer and winter) and Paralympic events. I asked lots of questions of the athletes before and after their events. As a U.S. Olympic champion and Hall of Famer, I had easy access and rapport with many of the nation's heroes and heroines.

In addition to meeting and interviewing a wide variety of Olympians, I found myself involved in various other Olympic-related endeavors: as a board member on the 1984 Los Angeles Olympic Organizing Committee, a television sports quiz show host, two terms as the president of the U.S. Olympians and Paralympians Association (an alumni organization), and chair of three Olympic-related foundations. I have written two books on the Olympics and co-authored two others. I've carried the Olympic flame as part of four Olympic Torch Relays, and I was honored to carry the Olympic flag into the Opening Ceremony of the 1984 Olympic Games in Los Angeles. With each exposure, I picked up a little more Olympic history.

During my corporate speeches, to make my points, I'll include stories of many more famous and more recent Olympians than myself. In social gatherings, I'll try to liven up the dinner conversation with some Olympic esoterica I've gathered over time. I am proud to say that I have devoted my life to the Olympic movement for more than 45 years.

In 2019 I had the honor of touring the construction site of the new U.S. Olympic and Paralympic Museum in Colorado Springs, Colorado, and the pleasure of meeting the museum's new CEO, Christopher Liedel. After welcoming him to the Olympic and Paralympic family, I shared some of my trivia and even provided a few hints to pique his interest. Christopher enjoyed hearing the stories and invited me to assemble many of them into a book, which the museum would publish. Naturally, I jumped at the chance.

With that same spirit in mind, I have gathered these 100 questions (with hints and answers provided) for you to enjoy and share with others. I am especially proud of the ones marked with a "WOW" or an "UH-OH" because these stories help me make my favorite point: Olympic champions are not extraordinary people. We are ordinary people who have found a way to accomplish extraordinary results in the area of life that matters most to us. If I guessed correctly, you will be amazed by what you read.

If Olympians and Paralympians share one characteristic, it's that we are wonderfully competitive. Everybody loves to win, but Olympians and Paralympians hate to lose. Put a group of us in a room, or on a bus, and the Games begin all over again. Whether in card games, board games, video games, or Olympic Games, we are always looking to make a contest out of it. So here's a challenge: Read the book, and if you like the stories, share your favorite question with some of your friends. If they get stuck, share the hint at the bottom of the page, and then make them work for the answer. It's just like playing the game "20 questions." Let them ask 10 yes-or-no questions, and see if they can solve the puzzle. If they succeed, see if they don't feel as victorious as I did on the medal podium in Montreal.

In the Olympic spirit!

– JOHN NABER

Swimming, 1976, 4 gold medals, 1 silver, USOP Hall of Fame

• HISTORY OF THE OLYMPIC GAMES •

The First Olympiad (a four-year period) began with the first Games of the Modern Era, in 1896. Each subsequent Olympiad has carried its own roman numeral (as of 2028, I through XXXIV), even when the Games had to be canceled. In addition to the Olympiad, which features summer competitions, the Olympic Winter Games began in 1924. The two sets of Games were staggered in 1994, to allow Olympic competition every two years. The Paralympic Games were introduced in 1960, and as of 2002, all Olympic and Paralympic Games take place in the same city, weeks apart.

1894: Pierre de Coubertin revives the Olympic Games in Paris, France, on June 23.

1896: Games of the First (I) Olympiad take place in Athens, Greece.

1900: II Olympiad, Paris, France.

1904: III Olympiad, St. Louis, Missouri, in connection with the 1904 World's Fair.

1908: IV Olympiad, London, England; first Parade of Nations.

1912: V Olympiad, Stockholm, Sweden.

1913: The Olympic flag with five interlocking rings is created by Pierre de Coubertin.

1916: VI Olympiad, Berlin, Germany. Games are canceled because of World War I.

1920: VII Olympiad, Antwerp, Belgium. For the first time, an athlete takes the Olympic Oath during the Opening Ceremony; the Olympic flag appears for the first time.

1924: I Winter Games, Helsinki, Finland. **VIII Olympiad,** Paris, France. The Olympic motto, *"Citius, Altius, Fortius"* ("Faster, Higher, Stronger"), is introduced.

1928: II Winter Games, St. Moritz, Switzerland. **IX Olympiad,** Amsterdam, Holland.

1932: III Winter Games, Lake Placid, New York. **X Olympiad,** Los Angeles, California; the Olympic Village is introduced.

1936: IV Winter Games, Garmisch-Partenkirchen, Germany. **XI Olympiad,** Berlin, Germany; first Olympic Torch Relay, first television coverage (closed circuit).

1937: Baron Pierre de Coubertin dies in Geneva, Switzerland.

1940: The Winter Games scheduled for Sapporo, Japan, and the **XII Olympiad,** first in Tokyo, then in Helsinki, Finland, are canceled because of World War II.

1944: The Winter Games in Cortina d'Ampezzo, Italy, and the **XIII Olympiad** in London, England, are canceled because of World War II.

1948: V Winter Games, St. Moritz, Switzerland. **XIV Olympiad,** London, England; first live broadcast television coverage (in London area). Stoke Mandeville Games (precursor to the Paralympic Games) also take place in London.

1952: VI Winter Games, Oslo, Norway. **XV Olympiad,** Helsinki, Finland.

1956: VII Winter Games, Cortina d'Ampezzo, Italy; first international (but Europe only) broadcasting coverage. **XVI Olympiad,** Melbourne, Australia.

1960: VIII Winter Games, Squaw Valley, California; first live television coverage in the United States. **XVII Olympiad,** Rome, Italy. Rome also hosted the first Paralympic Games.

1964: IX Winter Games, Innsbruck, Austria. **XVIII Olympiad,** Tokyo, Japan.

1968: X Winter Games, Grenoble, France. **XIX Olympiad**, Mexico City, Mexico; American medalists John Carlos and Tommie Smith demonstrate for civil rights on the medal podium.

1972: XI Winter Games, Sapporo, Japan. **XX Olympiad,** Munich, Germany; terrorists kill Israeli team; Title IX passes into law, providing women greater access to sporting opportunities.

1976: XII Winter Games, Innsbruck, Austria. **XXI Olympiad,** Montreal, Canada.

1978: The Amateur Sports Act is passed by U.S. Congress, giving USOC exclusive control of Olympic branding, images, and terminology in the United States.

1980: XIII Winter Games, Lake Placid, New York; "Miracle on Ice" U.S. hockey victory over Soviet Union. **XXII Olympiad,** Moscow, Russia; President Jimmy Carter and the United States lead a 65-nation boycott of the Games.

1984: XIV Winter Games, Sarajevo, Yugoslavia. **XXIII Olympiad,** Los Angeles, California; the Soviet Union leads 15 nations in a boycott of the Games; a record 140 nations participate; first profitable Games since 1932; organizer Peter Ueberroth is named *Time* magazine's "Person of the Year."

1986: IOC drops the term "amateur" from the Olympic Charter and removes ban on professional athletes.

1988: XV Winter Games, Calgary, Canada. **XXIV Olympiad,** Seoul, South Korea.

1992: XVI Winter Games, Albertville, France. **XXV Olympiad,** Barcelona, Spain; NBC TV has first pay-per-view triplecast; U.S. basketball team is nicknamed the "Dream Team"; South Africa returns to the Olympic family after ending apartheid policy; former Soviet nations compete as the Unified Team.

1994: XVII Winter Games, Lillehammer, Norway. First two-year hiatus from previous Games.

1996: Centennial Olympic Games in Atlanta, Georgia, U.S.A., are marred by a terrorist bomb.

1998: XVIII Winter Games, Nagano, Japan.

2000: XXVII Olympiad, Sydney, Australia.

2002: XIX Winter Games, Salt Lake City, Utah. Occur just months after the September 11, 2001, attacks.

2004: XXVIII Olympiad, Athens, Greece. NBCOlympics .com website is launched to feed live results and broadcast schedules.

2006: XX Winter Games, Turin, Italy.

2008: XXIX Olympiad, Beijing, China. First high-definition broadcast.

2010: XXI Winter Games, Vancouver, Canada.

2012: XXX Olympiad, London, England.

2014: XXII Winter Games, Sochi, Russia. IOC sells NBC domestic rights for the 2022–2032 Games for a reported $7.65 billion.

2016: XXXI Olympiad, Rio de Janeiro, Brazil.

2018: XXIII Winter Games, PyeongChang, South Korea.

2020: XXXII Olympiad, Tokyo, Japan, are postponed to 2021 because of the worldwide Covid-19 pandemic.

2022: XXIV Winter Games, Beijing, China. First city to host Games in both summer and winter.

2024: XXXIII Olympiad, Paris, France.

2026: XXV Winter Games, Milan and Cortina d'Ampezzo, Italy.

2028: XXXIV Olympiad, Los Angeles, California.

HISTORY

Q: In what sport did an Olympian with polio (and no use of legs and feet) win an Olympic silver medal?

Hint:

The competitor had to be lifted onto the field of play.

A: Equestrian dressage

Danish rider Lis Hartel on her horse, Jubilee, during the 1952 Olympic Summer Games in Helsinki, where she competed in equestrian dressage

Lis Hartel rode for Denmark in the 1952 and 1956 Olympic Games. Eight years prior to her first Olympic ride, while pregnant, she was stricken with polio that paralyzed almost her entire body. With therapy and help from her husband and mother, she was able to deliver her child and also recover the use of her arms and chest, but she remained unable to use her legs below the knees. Through will and determination, she found a way to use her thigh muscles to guide her horse, Jubilee, around the ring.

In 1948 Hartel's scores were good enough to qualify for the Olympic Games, but at the time women were not allowed to compete in Olympic equestrian events. By 1952 the gender ban was lifted, and Hartel became one of the first women to ride in the Olympic Games. Her silver-medal-winning performance in Helsinki was a major emotional moment. Not only did she need to be lifted onto her horse, but the eventual champion, Henri Saint Cyr of Sweden, lifted her off her horse and carried her onto the medal podium.

Two years later she was declared the winner at the unofficial world championships, and she was able to earn another silver medal at the 1956 Olympic Games. She also won the Danish National Championship seven times.

My Mum was determined to ride again, no matter what the doctors proposed.

—Pernille Siesbye, Lis Hartel's daughter

• STAT BOX •

Champions After Polio

U.S. Olympic & Paralympic Hall of Famers who overcame polio:

- Ray Ewry (track & field, 1900, 1908), 8 golds
- Tenley Albright (figure skating, 1952, 1956), 1 gold, 1 silver
- Wilma Rudolph (track & field, 1956, 1960), 3 golds, 1 bronze

Q: Which U.S. Olympic team Opening Ceremony flag bearer earned an Olympic gold medal while competing for another country?

Hint: Flag bearers for the United States are selected by the various sports' team captains and are usually chosen because of their long athletic careers.

A: Olga Fikotová-Connolly

Diplomatic relations between the United States and the Soviet Union were on fragile footing in the early 1950s, and often the conflict spilled over into sporting contests. At the 1956 Olympic Games in Melbourne, Australia, Olga Fikotová won the gold medal for Czechoslovakia in the women's discus. She defeated several Soviet throwers, and her margin of victory was more than 0.9 meters (3 ft). Because of the Soviet domination of Czechoslovakia, her willingness and ability to defeat athletes from the Soviet Union made her an American fan favorite. At the same Games, Hal Connolly, an American born with a defective left arm, won the gold medal in the hammer throw, defeating two Soviets by a little more than 15 centimeters (6 in).

Czechoslovakia's Olga Fikotová, making her record-breaking discus throw at the 1956 Games

During the Games the two champions began a relationship. When they married a year later, Olga Fikotová-Connolly was denied the right to compete for Czechoslovakia, so she would compete for the United States at four subsequent Olympic Games. At the 1972 Games in Munich, Germany, Fikotová-Connolly's American teammates elected her to carry the U.S. flag into the Opening Ceremony.

Romance at the Games

At the height of the Cold War with the Soviet Union, relations between individuals from both sides of the Iron Curtain were prohibited by the Communist authorities, but the romance between Connolly and Fikotová was praised by the rest of the world. Their marriage made international headlines and was celebrated by 40,000 people. The famous Czech runner Emil Zátopek served as best man. Connolly would hammer throw for the United States at three subsequent Olympic Games, and he held the world record for 10 years. Two of their children became national-caliber athletes. They divorced in 1975.

• STAT BOX •

Embraced by the United States

Athletes From Communist Countries:

- Vasily Alekseyev (weightlifting, 1972, 1976, Soviet Union)
- Olga Korbut (gymnastics, 1972, 1976, Soviet Union)
- Nadia Comaneci (gymnastics, 1976, 1980, Romania)
- Alberto Juantorena (track & field, 1976, Cuba)
- Katarina Witt (figure skating, 1984, 1988, 1994, East Germany)
- Sergey Bubka (track & field, 1988, 1992, 1996, 2000, Soviet Union, Ukraine)

From Other Countries:

- John Claude Killy (skiing, 1964, 1968, France)
- Michael Gross (swimming, 1984, 1988, Germany)
- Jayne Torvill and Christopher Dean (figure skating, 1980, 1984, 1994, Great Britain)
- Alberto Tomba (skiing, 1988, 1992, 1994, 1998, Italy)

Q: In what sport did a gold medalist's name get lost to the history books?

Hint:

The competitor was placed on the team just moments before the competition.

A: Rowing (pair-oared shell with coxswain)

The second modern Olympic Games took place in Paris, France, in 1900. In the coxed pair rowing competition, when the heavily favored Dutch team of Roelof Klein and François Brandt lost to a French boat in a qualifying heat, the Dutch decided to expel their heavier coxswain, Hermanus Brockmann, in favor of someone lighter.

At the time, the International Olympic Committee allowed athletes from multiple countries to share a boat, and the coxswain was primarily used for ballast. The Dutch had their eye on a boy who had been discarded earlier by the French team because he was too heavy (at 33 kilograms/72.5 lb).

They invited the youngster, who appeared to be around 10 years old, to hop into their boat. With this passenger, the Dutch pair won the gold medal and posed for pictures with the child, who then ran off into the crowd. Neither the youngster nor his age was ever identified. It is suspected that this boy might be the youngest competitor ever, but because three of the top four boats also had unidentified youngsters, the truth may never be known.

Dutch rowers François Brandt and Roelof Klein with unknown French coxswain, in the 1900 Summer Games in Paris

The original coxswain, 29-year-old Brockmann, went on to win a silver in the four-oared shell with coxswain event and a bronze medal in the eights.

Motivators!

Today, coxswains in rowing are much more than ballast. They are known as the motivators of the boat, shouting encouragement and position updates throughout the competition. Mary Whipple (left, bow) barked commands to the U.S. women in the 2004, 2008, and 2012 Olympic Games, leading the boats to one silver and two gold medals. When the U.S. women's eight was announced as the USOPC's Team of the Year in 2012, none of the ladies were present because they all were attending Whipple's wedding ceremony.

Q: Who was the first Olympian to appear on the front of the Wheaties cereal box?

Hint: Runner Jesse Owens and golfer Babe Didrikson and others did appear earlier on the side or back of the box, but not on the front.

A: Bob Richards

Bob Richards was a three-time Olympian. Ordained as a minister in 1946, with the nickname "Vaulting Vicar," he brought his evangelical passion to the promotion of health and fitness. After winning the Olympic bronze medal in 1948 and the gold in 1952 for pole vaulting, he became the first to successfully defend an Olympic pole vaulting gold medal in 1956. He also competed for the United States in the Olympic decathlon. In 1934 Wheaties cereal had begun using the slogan "Breakfast of Champions," placing pictures of great athletes on the side and back of the packaging. It was not until 1958, however, that the front of the box was dedicated to an athlete—and the first was Bob Richards. Richards had become a well-known figure, even appearing in 1957 on the television quiz show *What's My Line?* He soon became Wheaties' first official spokesperson, both for the cereal and for the creation of the Wheaties Sports Foundation, which promoted participation in Olympic sports. Later, Richards and his wife raised miniature horses on their ranch, called Olympian, in Gordon, Texas.

• STAT BOX •

Vaulting Stars

More than 60 U.S. Olympians have appeared on the front of the Wheaties box since 1958, including other pole vaulters:

- Bruce Jenner (decathlon, 1972, 1976)
- Dan O'Brien (decathlon, 1996)
- Stacy Dragila (pole vault, 2000)

U.S. pole vaulter Bob Richards (right) sets a new record in the 1952 Summer Games in Helsinki, Finland. Later, he would be the first Olympian to appear on the front of a box of Wheaties (above), called the "Breakfast of Champions."

Q: In what Olympic sport was there a three-way tie for the gold medal?

Hint: This has happened twice in Olympic history—in the same event!

A: Gymnastics (pommel horse, 1948 and 1988)

At the 1948 Games in London, three Finnish gymnasts received identical scores (38.70) in the pommel horse competition, and each was awarded the gold medal. Paavo Aaltonen won three gold medals and a bronze at those Games. Veikko Huhtanen won the all-around title that year, plus two more golds, a silver, and a bronze. Besides his 1948 gold, Heikki Savolainen won medals in four other Olympic Games, both before and after World War II. At the 1952 Games in Helsinki, at age 44, he was chosen to give the Olympic Oath during the Opening Ceremony.

At the 1988 Olympic Summer Games in Seoul, Bulgarian Lubomir Geraskov, above, wins gold on the pommel horse along with two others in a gymnastics tie.

Forty years later, at the 1988 Olympic Games in Seoul, South Korea, in the same pommel horse event, three gymnasts from three different countries obtained identical scores each of the three times they did their routines. In the compulsory exercises, Lubomir Geraskov (Bulgaria), Zsolt Borkai (Hungary), and Dmitri Bilozerchev (Soviet Union) each earned a 9.90. During the optional routines, each earned a 10.0. During the individual event finals, with the pressure on, all three delivered perfect performances, and all three tied to 1/1000 of a point with scores of 19.950. For Geraskov and Borkai, it would be their only medal of those Games. Bilozerchev also earned gold medals in the team and rings events, and finished third in the all-around.

• STAT BOX •

Breaking a Tie

Some rules for breaking a tie include the following:

- Weightlifting: Tie goes to the lightest athlete
- Archery: Shoot-off closest to the center
- Equestrian: Best cross-country score including faults and time penalties, followed by six other criteria
- Gymnastics: In individual event, best "execution" score; in all-around event, best three-event score
- Soccer: One overtime period followed by penalty kicks
- Track cycling: Lowest cumulated time in time-trial events
- Fencing: Coin flip for first advantage

The pommel horse is considered the most difficult event in men's gymnastics, requiring nerves of steel.

—Peter Vidmar (gymnastics, 1984, 2 gold medals, 1 silver)

Q: Only four Olympic host countries have been unable to win a single gold medal during their hosting period. Which country has the distinction of doing so twice?

Hint:

This country hosted both Summer and Winter Games.

Uh-Oh!

A: Canada, in Montreal, 1976, and in Calgary, 1988

The Canadian team marches in the Parade of Nations at the Opening Ceremony of the 1976 Olympic Games in Montreal.

The 1976 Summer Games in Montreal featured 21 sports and 169 events, but Canadian athletes were able to earn only five silver and six bronze medals. At the 1988 Games in Calgary, Canada's Brian Orser almost defeated American Brian Boitano for the gold in men's figure skating, and the host country had to settle for five total medals across 46 events in six sports.

In preparation for their third time hosting an Olympic Games—the 2010 Winter Games in Vancouver—the Canadian sporting authorities created the "Own the Podium" organization, dedicated to increasing Canada's medal output. Just two days after the Opening Ceremony, freestyle skier Alexandre Bilodeau (who finished 12th in 2006) struck gold in the men's moguls and earned Canada's first Olympic title on Canadian soil. Canadians went on to win a total of 26 medals and set a new record for gold medals—14—won by a nation in an Olympic Winter Games.

Three other countries have gone winless at home. The first Olympic Winter Games took place in Chamonix, France, in 1924, where 16 gold medals were awarded. The French athletes were unable to earn any of them. Four years later, the Games moved to St. Moritz, Switzerland, and again the host country was winless in 14 events. At the 1984 Winter Games in Sarajevo, the Yugoslav team won one silver medal in the 39 events contested; however, it was the first medal of any color won by Yugoslavia in a Winter Games.

For me, sport has been the school of life. That's where I've learned my discipline... that's how I've learned to deal with stress.

—Alex Bilodeau (freestyle skiing, 2006, 2010, 2014, 2 gold medals)

The Cherry on Top

In the 2010 Vancouver comeback, Canada won gold medals in team events including ice dance, women's two-man bobsled, men's short track speed skating relay, men's speed skating team pursuit, men's curling, and women's ice hockey. Perhaps the "cherry on top" (above) was Canadian National Hockey League favorite Sidney Crosby's winning goal against the U.S. team with seconds remaining in overtime of the Games' last event.

Q: Which city was the first to host an Olympic Games twice?

Hint: It will be the second city to host the Games three times.

A: Paris, France

Paris will host the Olympic Games for a third time in 2024.

French educator Baron Pierre de Coubertin was the founder of the modern Olympic Games, and at the first meeting of the International Olympic Committee (IOC) in 1894, it was decided to award the inaugural 1900 Games to Paris, France, to be held in conjunction with the 1900 World's Fair. Because IOC members did not want to wait for six years, in 1896 they allowed Athens, Greece, to host an Olympic Games. The 1900 Games took place over a five-month period, and many of the competitors did not know they were competing in an Olympic Games. Women competed in the Olympic Games for the first time that year, and 72 percent of the total competitors were French. The 1924 Games were again awarded to Paris in 1921, with 126 events taking place in 17 sports. It was the last Games under the IOC leadership of Baron de Coubertin. In the 21st century, Paris for a third time was called up to host the world in the summer of 2024—a hundred years after the city last hosted. Outside Paris, France hosted three Olympic Winter Games in three different cities: Chamonix in 1924, Grenoble in 1968, and Albertville in 1992.

Selecting a Host City

The IOC process for selecting a host city now has five basic parts: the "invitation phase," in which the IOC invites cities to learn about what it means to host Olympic and Paralympic Games; the two-year-long "candidature process," in which a city's infrastructure, weather, venue construction, hospitality offerings, security, government funding, and more are discussed; the "bid book" preparation, in which cities make their case for hosting the Games; the "vote," by IOC members; and the "contract signing" between the awardee and the IOC.

IOC president Thomas Bach and Los Angeles mayor Eric Garcetti with agreement for Los Angeles to host the 2028 Games

Q: In the 1936 Olympic Games in Berlin, the United States defeated Canada for the gold medal in basketball by a final score of 19–8. What was the reason for such a low-scoring game?

Hint:

At the half, the score was 15–4.

Uh-Oh!

A: The final was played outdoors on a clay court and in the rain.

Muddy basketball competition at the 1936 Summer Games in Berlin

The first time basketball enjoyed full medal status was at the 1936 Olympic Games in Berlin. That year, the International Basketball Federation (FIBA) elected to conduct the sport outdoors, and the local organizing committee chose to locate the competition in the tennis stadium on its reinforced clay courts, surrounded by a low brick wall.

American captain Bill Wheatley recalled that in those days, players used to shoot a larger, heavier ball with both hands. The inflatable bladder was laced up inside the leather ball with rawhide straps so the ball was never perfectly round. Dribbling was difficult even on dry ground.

The United States defeated Estonia (52–28), the Philippines (56–23), and Mexico (25–10) to reach the gold-medal game. A huge rainstorm flooded the court the day before the final, but the hosts insisted the tournament conclude on schedule. In the evening final against Canada, the air was cool (57°F/14°C) and the ground was wet and slippery in a drizzle. In the second half the skies opened up, and the court flooded. Wheatley said later, "We played two, 20-minute halves in front of 500 umbrellas, that I think had people under them."

The United States' center, Frank Lubin, said the officials had to suspend the double dribble rule because the ball could not bounce in five centimeters (2 in) of muddy water. Playing a very defensive game, each team scored only four points in the second half. Joe Fortenberry was the high scorer with eight points (equaling Canada's team total) in the lowest scoring basketball game in Olympic history.

Mexico defeated Poland (26–12) for the bronze. James Naismith, the inventor of the sport, awarded the medals to the winners.

U.S. Olympic Basketball Teams

The U.S. men's basketball teams have won 15 gold, one silver, and two bronze medals since the event was included in 1936. The U.S. women's basketball teams have won eight gold medals and one bronze (and one fourth place) since the event was included in 1976. Neither U.S. team participated in the 1980 Olympic Games.

The Dream Team's Scottie Pippen (8) and Clyde Drexler (10) at the 1992 Summer Games in Barcelona, Spain

Q: As of 2020, how many times has the United States hosted an Olympic Games?

Hint: **Don't forget to count the Olympic Winter Games.**

A: Eight times

The United States first hosted an Olympic Games in 1904, the year the World's Fair was held in St. Louis, Missouri. The International Olympic Committee allowed the Games to take place there simultaneously.

The 1932 Olympic Winter Games held in Lake Placid, New York, were opened by Franklin Delano Roosevelt less than a year before he was elected president. Months later, Los Angeles hosted the Summer Games and introduced the first athletes' village and medal podium.

The Games would not return to the United States until 1960, when they were awarded to Squaw Valley, California. The United States won its first Olympic hockey gold medal that year. Twenty years later, the hockey team would win again in what was called the "Miracle on Ice" when the 1980 Games returned to Lake Placid, New York.

Snowy mountains rise in the official poster of the VIII Olympic Winter Games, hosted by the United States in Squaw Valley, California, in 1960.

Los Angeles hosted the Games for the second time in 1984, and the United States won a record 83 gold medals. The Los Angeles organizers also created a successful financial model followed by most of the future Olympic Games. Atlanta, Georgia, hosted the 1996 Centennial Olympic Games, where the American women dominated in soccer, basketball, softball, and synchronized swimming.

In 2002 Salt Lake City, Utah, hosted the Games, with many of the 78 events taking place in nearby Park City. This marked the first time the Olympic Games and Paralympic Games were organized by the same committee. Los Angeles, California, has been awarded the right to host the Olympic Games in 2028.

1996 Explosion

The 1996 Centennial Olympic Games were marred by the detonation of a pipe bomb by an American terrorist inside Centennial Olympic Park, a popular meeting place for Olympic spectators.

The U.S. flag and flowers honor victims during a ceremony to reopen Olympic Park after the bombing attack at the Centennial Olympic Games in Atlanta, Georgia.

Q: Who and in what sport did a competitor represent their country in competition at various Olympic Games across a span of 48 years?

Hint:

In each appearance, the competitor shared the glory with a non-medal-eligible athlete.

A: Equestrian rider Hiroshi Hoketsu, from Japan, competed at the 1964 Games and again in 2008 and 2012.

Hiroshi Hoketsu competes for the Japanese mixed team in equestrian dressage at the 2008 Olympic Games in Beijing.

Equestrian Hiroshi Hoketsu was 23 years old when he qualified for his first Olympic Games, in Tokyo. After his 1964 participation, he would not make another team until 1988 but was then denied the chance to compete owing to legal restrictions placed on the animals. In the 2008 Beijing Games, 67-year-old Hoketsu was the oldest rider competing in dressage. Interviewed prior to the 2012 Olympic Games, he indicated that dressage was one of the few sports that would allow someone of his experience to continue competing at an elite level. And compete again he did, in the 2012 Games in London. At 71 years old, he was the oldest Olympic athlete ever to compete for Japan and the third-oldest Olympic competitor in history. Coincidentally, he finished 40th in his first Olympic appearance in 1964 and 41st in his last Olympic appearance in 2012.

It's unusual to see athletes compete in the Olympic Games after an eight-year absence, and even more rare after a 20-year absence. For Hoketsu to compete after a 44-year absence was truly amazing.

Having the Olympics return to Tokyo is deeply stirring. I want to attempt taking part as long as I have physical strength.

—Hiroshi Hoketsu
(equestrian dressage,
1964, 2008, 2012)

Age Is Just a Number

In 2008 American swimmer Dara Torres (below) won three medals in the 2008 Olympic Games in Beijing. It was her fifth Olympic Games, and at the age of 41, she became the oldest swimmer in history to win an Olympic medal. After her remarkable career, Torres wrote the memoir *Age Is Just a Number.*

Q: The highest honor an Olympian can receive from his/her teammates is to be chosen to carry their nation's flag into the Opening Ceremony. Only three American athletes have earned the honor *twice*. Who was the first?

Hint: This athlete was actually born outside the United States.

A: Pat McDonald carried the American flag into the 1920 and 1924 Olympic Games.

Around 1900 Patrick McDonald moved from Ireland to America, where he joined the New York Police Department, eventually directing traffic in Times Square. By 1907 he was six feet four inches (1.93 m) tall, weighed almost 300 pounds (136 kg), and was training for the 56-pound (25.4 kg) weight toss, using a heavy lead ball chained to a handle. That event was dropped from the 1908 Olympic program, so he focused on the 16-pound (7.26 kg) shot put. He won gold at the 1912 Games in Stockholm with an Olympic record of 15.34 meters and also won a silver in the since-discontinued "two-handed" shot put, where athletes take the best of three tosses from each hand added together. After World War I, at the 1920 Games in Antwerp, Belgium, as a returning Olympic champion, McDonald was asked to be America's standard-bearer for the Opening Ceremony. The 56-pound weight toss had been restored to the program and McDonald won his second gold medal. At age 42 he became—and remains—the oldest athlete ever to win an Olympic gold medal in track & field. At the 1924 Olympic Games in Paris, McDonald returned to the role of flag bearer at age 46. At age 53, he tossed the 56-pound weight just one foot (12 cm) shy of his Olympic record distance.

Irish American athlete Patrick Joseph "Pat" McDonald competed in three Olympic Games.

Chosen as the flag bearer, bobsledder James Bickford leads U.S. athletes into the 1956 Olympic Winter Games in Cortina, Italy.

Flag-bearing Honor

Two other Americans have been honored as two-time flag bearers. Four-time Olympic bobsledder James Bickford was selected for the Oslo Winter Games in 1952 and the Cortina Winter Games in 1956. Those same years, six-time Olympic fencer Norman Armitage was the U.S. team's choice to carry the flag at the Summer Games in Helsinki and Melbourne.

Q: The Olympic flame is carried into the Opening Ceremony after a long, international Torch Relay, then the flame burns inside the Olympic cauldron for the duration of the Games until it is extinguished at the end of the Closing Ceremony. How is the first torch of the Torch Relay ignited?

Hint:

It is not ignited by an "eternal flame" in Greece.

A: By the reflected rays of the sun

Every two years, approximately two months before the next Opening Ceremony, a crowd gathers in Olympia, Greece, at the site of the ancient Olympic Games, near the Temple of Hera. In a quasi-religious ceremony, actresses dressed as priests use a large parabolic mirror, like the reflective bowl that surrounds a flashlight bulb, to ignite the flame. The bowl is turned toward the sun, focusing its rays onto a single spot. The first torch of that year's relay is activated, slowly releasing a 15-minute supply of flammable gas. The head of the torch is then placed near the focal point, and the heat ignites the pressurized gas in the torch, lighting the flame. This flame is then carried by foot, boat, car, airplane, and other modes of transportation until it reaches the Opening Ceremony at the designated city, lighting the official Olympic cauldron. The torch is not passed from runner to runner. Instead, the flame is passed from torch to torch, which allows the runners to keep their torch as a memento of the occasion. This method also creates lots of opportunities for the flame to be accidentally extinguished. For this purpose, a backup flame is also captured and kept in a secure lantern that travels with the Torch Relay.

A traditional high priestess in Olympia, Greece, lights the Olympic flame from the rays of the sun, to be carried by a Torch Relay to the site of the Olympic Games.

Cauldron Malfunction

One of the most memorable moments in torch lighting history occurred at the 2000 Olympic Games in Sydney, Australia (left), when a mechanical device malfunctioned. The huge circular cauldron was ignited by the final torchbearer, rose overhead, and then failed to keep moving toward the top of the stadium because of a faulty safety warning. Dramatic music kept playing for what seemed like 10 minutes before two technicians, Peter Tait and Rob Ironside, reprogrammed the device, and the flame proceeded up the mechanical ramp to thunderous applause.

Q: Parts of the body of the founder of the modern Olympic movement are buried in two different places. Where are they?

Hint:

His body was divided at his request.

A: Pierre de Coubertin's body is buried in Lausanne, Switzerland, but his heart is buried in Olympia, Greece.

Pierre de Coubertin devoted much of his life to the Olympic movement, and he is buried in Lausanne, Switzerland, headquarters of the International Olympic Committee (IOC). According to his wishes, his heart was sent to Olympia, Greece, and it is now located in a commemorative pillar on the grounds of the International Olympic Academy. After the lighting of each Games' Torch Relay, the first runner always stops at the Coubertin Grove to pay homage to the founder.

Coubertin was a French aristocrat and educator who believed that sport is essential in the development of young men and women. In 1894 he proposed the creation of the Olympic Games of the modern era based on the ancient Games of Greece. This led to the creation of the IOC, which continues to oversee the modern Olympic Games. He became the IOC president shortly after the 1896 Games in Athens and held the position through the 1924 Olympic Games in Paris. The Pierre de Coubertin medal honors sportsmanship at the Olympic Games, and it is the highest award that the IOC can bestow.

Pierre de Coubertin's grave, Boix-de-Vaux Cemetery, Lausanne, Switzerland

Pierre de Coubertin, Poet

Pierre de Coubertin (above) won an Olympic gold medal for literature at the 1912 Olympic Games in Stockholm, Sweden, for his poem "Ode to Sport," which he submitted under a pseudonym. Also, de Coubertin summarized the Olympic ideal in his quote: "The important thing in life is not the triumph but the struggle, the essential thing is not to have conquered but to have fought well."

"Citius, Altius, Fortius" ("Faster, Higher, Stronger")

—Pierre de Coubertin's official motto of the Olympic Games

Q: In what sport did an American athlete earn a place on six consecutive U.S. Olympic teams, winning a medal each and every time?

Hint: The athlete was 16 years old when she earned her first Olympic medal.

A: Shooting

Already an Olympic medalist in five Olympic Games, U.S. shooter Kim Rhode prepares for the 2016 Games in Rio de Janeiro, where she will medal again.

Kim Rhode was raised in a family that regularly used guns on hunting trips, and she quickly learned to shoot. She began competing before her 11th birthday and won her first world championship at age 13. In 1996 she was the youngest member of the U.S. shooting team in Atlanta, where she earned her first Olympic medal, a gold in the double trap. In 2000, in Sydney, she finished third (bronze) in double trap and seventh in skeet. Rhode returned to win gold in double trap and finish fifth in skeet at the 2004 Games in Athens. At the 2008 Games in Beijing, she claimed the silver medal in skeet. In the 2012 Olympic Games in London, she once again stood on the top medal platform, earning her third Olympic gold medal, becoming the only U.S. competitor ever to win individual medals at five Olympic Games. Four years later, she medaled again, making her the first U.S. athlete in any sport to win medals in six consecutive Olympic Games and the first Olympian of either gender to win Olympic medals on five different continents. Rhode trains in California while also raising a young child. She claims to want to compete well into her 70s, hoping to break the mark for the oldest Olympic champion on record.

When you hit a target and the crowd cheers, it's an amazing thing.

—Kim Rhode
(shooting, 1996, 2000, 2004, 2008, 2012, 2016,
3 gold medals, 1 silver, 2 bronzes)

• STAT BOX •

Shooting Events

As a result of changes made in 2018 by the International Shooting Sport Federation, the 2021 Olympic shooting events will include five events for each of the three different weapons (rifle, pistol, and shotgun), and an equal number of medals for each gender:

- 10-meter air rifle: Men, women, and teams
- 50-meter rifle: Three positions for men and women
- 10-meter air pistol: Men, women, and teams
- 25-meter pistol: Men and women
- Trap shooting: Men, women, and teams
- Skeet shooting: Men and women

Q: In what sport did a father/son pair compete together in three different Olympic Games?

Hint: The father is the current record holder for the oldest Olympic champion as well as the oldest Olympic competitor. He and his son have earned a combined 15 Olympic medals.

A: Shooting

Swedish shooting team Alfred Swahn, Oscar Swahn, Åke Lundeberg, and Per-Olof Arvidsson won gold at the 1912 Olympic Games.

Oscar Swahn competed at his first Olympic Games (London, 1908) at the age of 61, alongside his son, Alfred. Oscar earned two gold medals and one bronze, and shared the team gold with his son. Four years later, at the Stockholm Games in their home country, Oscar won gold and bronze, becoming at 64 years and 258 days of age the oldest Olympic champion in history. In the same Games, Alfred earned two more gold medals. The 1916 Olympic Games were canceled because of World War I, but in 1920 the pair returned to earn four medals—three silvers, one bronze—between them. At 72 years and 280 days of age, Oscar became the oldest Olympic competitor and oldest Olympic medalist on record. Alfred competed without his father in Paris in 1924, where he won three more medals—one silver and two bronzes.

• STAT BOX •

Twin Champions

Ten pairs of twins have competed for the United States in the same Olympic sport:

- Phil (Alpine skiing, 1980, 1984) and Steve Mahre (Alpine skiing, 1976, 1984)
- Karen and Sarah Josephson (synchronized swimming, 1988, 1992)
- David and James Hazewinkle (wrestling, 1968, 1972)
- Ed and Lou Banach (wrestling, 1984)
- Jocelyne and Monique Lamoureux (ice hockey, 2010, 2014, 2018)
- Paul and Morgan Hamm (gymnastics, 2000, 2004)
- Tyler and Cameron Winklevoss (rowing, 2008)
- Bob and Mike Bryan (tennis, 2008, 2012)
- Alvin and Calvin Harrison (track & field, 1996, 2000)
- Robert and Randy Dean (team handball, 1976)

Q: In what sport did a competitor represent their country on 10 Olympic teams?

Hint:

The number might have been 11 had the athlete's home country not withdrawn from the 1980 "Boycott Games" in Moscow.

A: Equestrian

Canada's Ian Millar rides Star Power in the 2012 Olympic Games jumping event.

Ian Millar was first invited to join the Canadian equestrian team in 1971, and in that capacity he and his horses have appeared in 10 Olympic jumping competitions—more than any other athlete from any sport. It might have been 11, but Canada joined the United States in the boycott of the 1980 Games in Moscow.

Millar's first Olympic appearance was in Munich in 1972. Later nicknamed "Captain Canada," he won his first Olympic medal—a silver—at the 2008 Beijing Games at the age of 61. In 2012 he made his final Olympic appearance at the Games in London. He might have joined his daughter on the Rio team in 2016, but his horse was unfit. In Olympic competition, he earned nine top 10 finishes.

Midway through his career, Millar was inducted into the Canadian Sports Hall of Fame in 1996, thanks in part to Pan-American competitions where he won 10 medals—four golds, four silvers, and two bronzes. Millar retired from active competition after 2016 and now trains horses and coaches riders. Millar and his family own and operate Millar Brooke Farm in Perth, Ontario.

To ride on a team at the Olympics is the ultimate experience, because at the Olympics, everybody watches.

—Ian Millar
(equestrian jumping, 1972, 1976, 1984, 1988, 1992, 1996, 2000, 2004, 2008, 2012, 1 silver medal)

Equestrian Events

In Olympic equestrian team and individual events, the top three scores count. The events include dressage—testing the level of training for horse and rider; show jumping—over obstacles inside the ring; and eventing—a combination of dressage, jumping, and cross-country jumping. Men and women compete as equals. Another Olympic event that includes animals is the show jumping portion of the modern pentathlon.

A Swedish horse and rider take a jump during the 2012 Olympic Games in London.

Q: In what sport did an international (not U.S. born) individual win an Olympic gold medal the first time ever attempting the event?

Hint: The winner had already earned two gold medals in the sport at the same Games.

A: Track & field

In less than four years of competition, Czech runner Emil Zátopek was setting national records for the 2,000-, 3,000-, and 5,000-meter runs. At the 1948 Olympic Games in London, he earned gold in the 10,000 meters and silver in the 5,000 meters. Over the next four years, he would break the 10,000-meter world record five times. At the 1952 Olympic Games in Helsinki, he crushed the fields in the 5,000- and 10,000-meter runs, setting Olympic records in both. Coincidentally, Zátopek's wife, Dana Zátopková, also won a gold medal and set a new Olympic record in the javelin throw at the 1952 Games.

Czech Olympic champions runner Emil Zátopek and his wife, javelin thrower Dana Zátopková, with their four gold medals from the 1952 Summer Games (left); Zátopek's marathon win (right)

After Zátopek won his second gold medal in Helsinki, he decided to try his luck in the marathon, a 42.19-kilometer (26.2 mi) run in which he had never competed. The race took place three days later, and Zátopek pulled away from the field around the 15-kilometer (9.3 mi) mark and ended up winning the race by more than 2.5 minutes. He is the only person to win those three events in the same Olympic Games.

Zátopek tried to defend his marathon title in 1956, but an earlier injury prevented him from finishing higher than sixth place. In 1975 the International Olympic Committee presented Zátopek with the Pierre de Coubertin medal, its highest award. In 2013 *Runner's World* magazine selected him as the "Greatest Runner of All Time."

• STAT BOX •

Olympic Partners

These Olympic champions married other Olympic champions:

- Olga Fikotová (track & field, 1956, 1960, 1964, 1968, 1972) and Harold Connolly (track & field, 1956, 1960, 1964, 1968)
- Roland Matthes (swimming, 1968, 1972, 1976) and Kornelia Ender (swimming, 1972, 1976)
- Bart Conner (gymnastics, 1976, 1980, 1984) and Nadia Comaneci (gymnastics, 1976, 1980)
- Jason Kenny (cycling, 2008, 2012, 2016) and Laura Trott (cycling, 2012, 2016)
- Steffi Graf (tennis, 1988) and Andre Agassi (tennis, 1996)
- Matt Emmons (shooting, 2004, 2008, 2012, 2016) and Katerina Kurková (shooting, 2004, 2008)

Q: Who is the only athlete to win Olympic medals in running, jumping, and throwing events?

Hint:

This athlete is mostly remembered as a successful competitive golfer.

A: Mildred "Babe" Didrikson Zaharias

U.S. track & field champion Babe Didrikson's winning javelin throw at the 1932 Summer Games in Los Angeles (above); left, the 1981 postage stamp honoring her lifetime athletic achievements

Considered one of the finest athletes of all time, Babe Didrikson excelled in basketball, baseball, golf, diving, roller skating, bowling, and track & field. She single-handedly won the 1932 national Amateur Athletic Union (AAU) Team Championship when she won more than half of the 10 events. At the 1932 Olympic Games in Los Angeles, Didrikson won golds and set the world record running the 80-meter hurdles and the Olympic record throwing the javelin. She tied the world record and the eventual gold medalist in the high jump but was ruled the silver medalist for using what was deemed "improper form."

Her post-Olympic golf career was equally accomplished. She won 82 tournaments and even qualified for the final two rounds in two (male) Professional Golfers' Association (PGA) events without using a sponsor exemption (something done by no other woman to date). She helped create the LPGA (Ladies Professional Golf Association), and in 1950 she won the Grand Slam (all three major tournaments in her sport in one calendar year). Her likeness was featured on a U.S. postage stamp in 1981, and in 1983 she was inducted into the U.S. Olympic Hall of Fame.

The formula for success is simple: practice and concentration, then more practice and more concentration.

—Babe Didrikson Zaharias (track & field, 1932, 2 gold medals, 1 silver)

• STAT BOX •

Postage Stamp Honorees

Other Olympians who have appeared on U.S. postage stamps:

- Duke Kahanamoku (swimming, 1912, 1920, 1924)
- Jesse Owens (track & field, 1936), on various stamps
- Eddie Egan (boxing, 1920; bobsled, 1932)
- Ray Ewry (track & field, 1900, 1904, 1908)
- Helene Madison (swimming, 1932)
- Hazel Wightman (tennis, 1924)
- Jim Thorpe (track & field, 1912)
- Wilma Rudolph (track & field, 1956, 1960)
- Muhammad Ali (boxing, 1960)

Q: Who was America's first female flag bearer in an Olympic Opening Ceremony?

Hint:

She was the first woman ever to compete in six Olympic Games.

A: Janice-Lee Romary

Led by their flag bearer, fencer Janice-Lee Romary, the U.S. team marches in the Parade of Nations during the Opening Ceremony of the 1968 Games in Mexico City.

Romary learned how to fence at a workshop for stage and screen actors managed by her father in Hollywood. Her first Olympic appearance was in the 1948 Olympic Games in London while she was a student at the University of Southern California. In 1950 she won her first of what would become 10 national titles (still a record). She returned to the Olympic Games in 1952, 1956, 1960, 1964, and finally in 1968 in Mexico City.

Al Oerter (track & field, 1956, 1960, 1964, 1968) was invited by the U.S. Olympic leadership to carry the American flag into the 1968 Opening Ceremony but demurred, instead suggesting that Romary be honored in his place. There was some resistance at the U.S. Olympic Committee, but they finally relented and Romary became the first woman to carry the Stars and Stripes into an Olympic Opening Ceremony.

Last…then First

When Nigeria elected not to send their fencer to the 2004 Games in Athens, a slot was open. As the next ranked sabre fencer in the world, American Mariel Zagunis was invited. She had been, quite literally, the last kid chosen for the U.S. team, yet her Athens performance won America's first fencing gold medal in 100 years. The daughter of two Olympic rowers, Zagunis successfully defended her crown in 2008 (Beijing), leading the U.S. sabre team to a bronze medal. She was chosen as the U.S. flag bearer for the Opening Ceremony in 2012. She did not win a medal then, but she earned another team medal in 2016.

American fencer Mariel Zagunis, who won gold in 2004 and bronze in 2008, leads the U.S. team in the Opening Ceremony of the 2012 Games in London.

Q: Charlie Pond was inducted into the Halls of Fame of four different sports. What four Olympic sports/disciplines have benefited from Pond's contributions?

Hint: He was not an Olympic athlete, but his invention greatly assisted athletes in all four sports, both Winter and Summer.

A: Gymnastics, diving, freestyle skiing, and trampolining/acrobatics

Charlie Pond coaches Dickie Browning to make a tumbling pass over a high jump bar set above the existing world record.

Before World War II, gymnast Charlie Pond, while trying to master a difficult twisting somersault, crashed on his landing and realized that he needed more help to practice difficult moves than a good coach could provide. Years later, he watched circus acrobats practicing on a trampoline and saw the value of this technology in learning new skills. During World War II, in the South Pacific, Pond and his platoon came under sniper fire, and he jumped into a foxhole. While ducking his head and waiting for help, his mind went back to the time he landed poorly in the gymnasium. It dawned on him that a belt around the waist of a tumbler could be improved if it also could twist. He imagined two leather belts separated by ball bearings: The inner belt would go around the waist of the gymnast and the outer belt would be suspended from overhead by ropes that could be pulled by a coach, lifting the tumbler into the air in order to practice multiple spinning somersaults. This innovative technology was instrumental in helping gymnasts, divers, freestyle skiers and trampoline acrobats.

• STAT BOX •

Hi-Tech Games

Other innovative technologies in Olympic sport:

- Composite vaulting poles
- Video instant replay in diving
- Laser handguns in modern pentathlon
- Electronic scoring in fencing
- Vaulting table and loaded floors in gymnastics
- Compressed air release in diving
- Foam landing pits in track & field
- Rowing ergometer

Charlie Pond's belt helped gymnasts and other athletes become world champions.

Benefit of the Belt

After the war, Pond put his idea into practice while working as the gymnastics coach at the Dallas Athletic Club. Benefiting from the belt, one of Pond's students, Richard "Dickie" Browning, was able to complete a tumbling pass that launched him over a high jump bar set five centimeters (2 in) above the existing world record. Another Pond protégé, Dickie's brother, David "Skippy" Browning, won the 1946 world title on the trampoline and the 1952 Olympic gold medal in springboard diving in pool competitions. In the 1970s Pond began coaching freestyle skiing athletes. Frankie Bare, Jr., the son of one of Pond's earlier gymnastic students, became the first man to successfully land a quadruple somersault with three twists on skis.

Q: Double gold medalist James Snook was on the U.S. 30-meter and 50-meter military pistol teams, both of which earned gold in the 1920 Games in Antwerp. Years later he was executed in the electric chair for murder. What weapons did he use to commit the crime of murder?

The crime occurred at a shooting range, but the murder weapon was not a gun.

A: He used a ball-peen hammer and a pocketknife to kill his mistress.

James Snook, top row second from right, and the U.S. men's shooting team at the 1920 Olympic Games in Antwerp, Belgium

James Snook was one of four members to compete on both shooting teams in 1920—the last year those events appeared on the Olympic program. He had graduated from Ohio State University in 1908 as a veterinarian and later led their department of veterinary medicine. He also invented the "Snook hook," a sharp surgical instrument for spaying animals.

Nine years after his Olympic triumphs, Snook was arrested for the murder of Theora Hix, a 24-year-old medical student with whom he was having an affair. Snook testified that during a tryst at a shooting range, she had threatened to harm his family with a gun he had provided for her protection. It was later determined that he hit her on the head with a ball-peen hammer and cut her throat with the precision of a surgeon. Blood was found on his hammer and pocketknife.

The jury took less than 30 minutes to reach a conviction. He was electrocuted at the Ohio State Penitentiary on February 28, 1930.

Ohio Professor and His Co-ed Victim

DR. JAMES H. SNOOK

THEORA HIX

James Snook's 1929 murder of his mistress made news across the nation, including in North Dakota's *Bismarck Tribune*.

Inventive Olympian

At the 1908 Olympic Games in London, two Americans tied for the gold medal in the pole vault. Edward Cook and Alfred Carlton Gilbert both cleared the bar at 3.71 meters (12 ft 2 in). In 1913 Gilbert, whose talents included magician and toymaker, developed the Erector set for aspiring young builders. The toy set included lightweight construction metal beams that could be connected by nuts and bolts, pulleys, gears, wheels, and levers. By 1935 more than 30 million sets had been sold worldwide.

U.S. Olympic gold medalist and inventor Alfred Carlton Gilbert

Q: During the Opening Ceremony of the 1984 Olympic Games in Los Angeles, the International Olympic flag was carried into the stadium by a group of 10 Olympians and one individual who had never competed in the Olympic Games. Who was this non-Olympian?

Hint: His grandfather was one of the greatest athletes of all time!

A: Bill Thorpe, Jr., the grandson of Jim Thorpe, the 1912 double gold medalist

Bill Thorpe, Jr., left, and Gina Hemphill, right, begin the 1984 Olympic Torch Relay on American soil.

Jim Thorpe might be the greatest American athlete ever. Not only did he win the 5-event pentathlon (since discontinued) and the 10-event decathlon at the 1912 Olympic Games in Stockholm, he also played professional football (inducted into the Professional Football Hall of Fame), baseball (member of the 1913 National League Champion New York Giants), basketball, lacrosse, and even won an intercollegiate ballroom dancing competition in 1912.

At the 1912 Olympic team tryouts, his performance in the pentathlon was so overwhelming that he was not required to compete for a spot in the decathlon. His victory in the Olympic decathlon was the first and only time he competed in the event, and the Olympic record he set would last almost 20 years.

In the year following his gold medals in Stockholm, reports surfaced that Thorpe had played in a couple of semiprofessional baseball games, invalidating the required amateur status. His Olympic medals and titles were stripped from him by the International Olympic Committee (IOC).

In 1983 the IOC was convinced to posthumously reinstate Thorpe's medals and make him a co-champion with the men he had defeated over half a century before. His children, Gale and Bill, were presented with commemorative medallions to mark the occasion. Additionally, Thorpe's grandson, Bill Jr., was one of the first runners to carry the 1984 Olympic flame (along with Jesse Owens's granddaughter, Gina Hemphill), and Bill was also invited to honor his grandfather by joining favored local Olympians as a bearer of the white Olympic flag during the 1984 Opening Ceremony.

• STAT BOX •

1984 Ceremony Participants

Flag bearers and escorts at the 1984 Los Angeles Olympic Games Opening Ceremony:

- Al Oerter (track & field, 1956, 1960, 1964, 1968)
- Billy Mills (track & field, 1960)
- Bruce Jenner (decathlon, 1972, 1976)
- John Naber (swimming, 1976)
- Mack Robinson (track & field, 1936)
- Parry O'Brien (track & field, 1952, 1956, 1960, 1964)
- Patty McCormick (diving, 1952, 1956)
- Richard Sandoval (boxing, 1980)
- Sammy Lee (diving, 1948, 1952)
- Wyomia Tyus (track & field, 1964, 1968)
- Bill Thorpe, Jr.

Q: What two Olympic Winter Games sports have also appeared in the Olympic Summer Games?

Hint: They are usually the two most popular sports of the Olympic Winter Games.

A: Ice hockey and figure skating

Before the first Olympic Winter Games in Chamonix, France, in 1924, winter and summer sports had to coexist on the Olympic program. At the 1908 Games in London, figure skating took place six months after most of the other sports had competed. That year's figure skating gold medals went to Ulrich Salchow (Sweden), Madge Syers (Great Britain), and Anna Hübler and Heinrich Burger (Germany). Additionally, Nikolai Panin (Russian Empire) won a gold in the now discontinued "Special Figures" event. Although figure skating was the first winter sport included in the Olympic Games, it was not on the program in the next Games, in 1912 in Stockholm.

German figure skating pair Anna Hübler and Heinrich Burger win gold at the 1908 Olympic Games in London.

In 1920 the Olympic Games were in Antwerp, Belgium, and in addition to figure skating, ice hockey was added to the program. This Olympic ice hockey tournament was also the first world championship in that sport. Canada won the gold, with the United States and Czechoslovakia earning the silver and bronze, respectively. In figure skating, the individual gold medals went to the Swedes, Gillis Grafström and Magda Mauroy-Julin, and the Finnish pair, Ludowika and Walter Jakobsson.

Four years later, the first Olympic Winter Games took place in Chamonix, France, and, in addition to these two sports, seven others were added to the program.

• STAT BOX •

First Winter Games

Sports and disciplines in the 1924 Olympic Winter Games:

- Bobsled
- Curling
- Ice hockey
- Figure skating
- Speed skating
- Cross-country skiing
- Ski jumping
- Nordic combined
- Military patrol

Once an Olympian, Always an Olympian; Never Former, Never Past

—Motto, U.S. Olympians and Paralympians Association

Q: In what sport did a world-class athlete who had lost their dominant hand to an explosive device win an Olympic title using the other hand?

Hint: The athlete not only won gold, but four years later successfully defended the title.

A: Shooting (25-meter rapid fire pistol)

Right-handed Hungarian Army sergeant Károly Takács was denied the chance to compete in the 1936 Olympic Games because only commissioned officers were allowed to represent their country in shooting events at that time. When that rule was lifted, Takács looked to the 1940 Olympic Games as his first opportunity, until a faulty grenade exploded in a 1938 training accident and badly injured his shooting hand. Undaunted, Takács trained in secret, holding his pistol in his left hand. Just one year later, he amazed his countrymen when he was able to win the national championship with his nondominant hand. The next two Olympic Games were canceled because of World War II, so it was not until the 1948 Olympic Games in London (10 years after his accident) that Takács had the opportunity to win his first Olympic medal.

Carlos Enrique Díaz Sáenz Valiente, the 1947 world champion from Argentina, was surprised to see Takács in the contest, and even more surprised when Takács won. Four years later, at the Games in Helsinki, Takács became the first man to successfully defend an Olympic 25-meter rapid fire pistol title.

Using his nondominant left hand, Hungarian shooter Károly Takács won gold at the 1948 Olympic Games in London.

• STAT BOX •

Heroes With Handicaps

U.S. Olympic competitors with physical handicaps include the following:

- Cliff Meidl (canoe/kayak, 1996, 2000), severe electric burns to both knees
- Greg Barton (canoe/kayak, 1984, 1988, 1992), born with club feet
- Jim Abbott (baseball, 1988), born with one hand
- Jeff Float (swimming, 1984), deaf from viral meningitis
- Marla Runyan (track & field, 2000), degenerative retina condition leading to blindness
- Norman Armitage (fencing, 1928, 1932, 1936, 1948, 1952, 1956), chemical burns
- Glen Cunningham (track & field, 1936), badly burned legs

You've got to take your limitations and turn them into strengths.

—Cliff Meidl
(canoe/kayak, 1996, 2000, flag bearer 2000)

Q: In what sport did America's first female Olympic champion not even know she'd won the Olympic competition?

Hint:

She wasn't aware because she didn't know she was competing in the Olympic Games.

Uh-Oh!

A: Golf

A Charles Dana Gibson portrait of Margaret Abbott, an American visiting Paris in 1900 who, on a whim, entered the first Olympic golf tournament for women—and won

The 1900 Olympic Games took place in connection with the Paris World's Fair, and the sporting events stretched across a six-month period. Margaret Abbott and her mother, Mary, were living in Paris at the time and, on a whim, they both entered what they thought was merely "an International Tournament." Margaret's score was a respectable 47 strokes for nine holes and she was awarded a porcelain bowl for her prize. It was not until years after her death that her family learned that her accomplishment made her America's first female Olympic champion.

In addition, Margaret's mother, Mary, who finished seventh in the tournament, is the only mother to join her daughter competing in the same Olympic event in the same Games.

• STAT BOX •

First Olympic Sports for Women

Women competed in these sports at the 1900 Olympic Games:

- Tennis
- Sailing
- Croquet
- Equestrian
- Golf

Your mother was the first [female] American Olympic champion.

—Historian Paula D. Welch to Margaret Abbott's son

A Gold First

Alice Coachman was raised in the segregated South, and because of her color she was denied access to proper equipment and entry into many of the local sporting events. But at the 1948 Olympic Games in London, she won the high jump and became the first African American woman to win Olympic gold. In 2004, Coachman was inducted into the U.S. Olympic and Paralympic Hall of Fame."

American Alice Coachman sets an Olympic record with her high jump at the 1948 Games in London.

Q: Why did New York Yankees owner George Steinbrenner pay for an Olympian's post-athletic medical degree?

Hint:

The instigating event happened at the 1992 Games in Barcelona, when Steinbrenner was a vice president of the U.S. Olympic Committee.

The father of one of America's swimmers passed away from a heart attack in the stadium during the Opening Ceremony, and Steinbrenner wanted to help the aspiring doctor attain a medical diploma.

In 1989 George Steinbrenner, then a vice president of the U.S. Olympic Committee, was charged with spearheading an investigation into why the U.S. Olympic team at the 1988 Winter Games had performed below expectations. The Steinbrenner Report produced a wide range of recommendations, including the need to provide financial grants to Olympic hopefuls. Steinbrenner took a personal interest in dozens of America's athletes, providing his own funds to aid in their training. At the 1992 Olympic Games in Barcelona, he was present to deliver the sad news to swimmer Ron Karnaugh that Karnaugh's father suffered a heart attack in the stadium during the Opening Ceremony and died on the scene. Karnaugh did swim the 200-meter individual medley in those Games and finished a respectable sixth place.

Karnaugh was scheduled to begin medical school one month after the Games, and Steinbrenner offered to pay his entire tuition. Karnaugh later said that Steinbrenner helped fill a fatherly void in his life.

• STAT BOX •

Olympic Generosity

Some other U.S. Olympians helped financially by Steinbrenner:

- Michelle Kwan (figure skating, 1998, 2002)
- Trent Dimas (gymnastics, 1992)
- Nicole Bobeck (figure skating, 1998)
- Tonya Harding (figure skating, 1992, 1994)
- Diane Dixon (track & field, 1984, 1988)

American Ron Karnaugh in the men's 200-meter individual medley swim trials before Sydney's 2000 Olympic Summer Games

Q: In what event did an athlete win an Olympic gold medal for performance while under the influence of multiple doses of strychnine?

Hint:

This athlete was not the first competitor to cross the finish line.

Uh-Oh!

A: Marathon

Attendants at the 1904 Olympic marathon in St. Louis, Missouri, help ailing runner Thomas Hicks during his gold-medal victory.

The marathon (42.19 kilometers/26.2 mi) at the 1904 Olympic Games in St. Louis took place on a hot, humid, and dusty course. While 32 competitors entered the race, only 14 would finish. The runners followed a caravan of automobiles carrying officials, doctors, and journalists.

One runner was chased off course by angry dogs and others fell ill because of the dust or eating unripe apples along the way. Other runners took naps mid-race or just gave up.

Around the 25.7-kilometer (16 mi) mark, Thomas Hicks, a brass worker from Cambridge, Massachusetts, enjoyed a 2.4-kilometer (1.5 mi) lead on the field but was beginning to fatigue. His handlers administered a small dose of strychnine sulfate mixed with raw egg white. In the early 1900s this drug was believed to help a variety of ailments, but today it is mainly used as rat poison. A few kilometers later, Hicks received another dose. Just 3.2 kilometers (2 mi) before the finish, on an uphill grade, Hicks slowed to a walk and additional doses (mixed with brandy) were given. He finished the race a few minutes ahead of his closest competitor and almost collapsed across the finish line, where he was promptly treated by doctors.

While Hicks had been running ahead, another U.S. competitor, Fred Lorz, jumped in an automobile 17.5 kilometers (11 mi) down the route and was driven close to the finish, where he ran into the stadium 15 minutes before Hicks arrived. He was almost awarded the title, but Lorz admitted to his prank before the gold medal was presented.

Hicks continued to run, winning a race in Chicago in 1906 and finishing another in 1909. Lorz won the Boston Marathon in 1905.

U.S. marathoner Frank Shorter won gold in the 1972 Olympic Games in Munich.

Gold Despite Imposters

At the 1972 Games in Munich, American Frank Shorter led the marathon. As he neared the stadium, a German student in running gear jumped a barricade and ran toward the finish line. He was eventually apprehended, and Shorter claimed the gold. In 1976 Shorter won a silver medal behind an East German who took gold but was suspected of cheating. Some say that Shorter won twice and twice finished behind an imposter.

Q: Who are the three women tied for the honor of America's most decorated female Olympian?

Hint:

Each has 12 Olympic medals in the same sport, and their careers overlapped.

Dara Torres (1984, 1988, 1992, 2000, 2008, 4 golds, 4 silvers, 4 bronzes), Jenny Thompson (1992, 1996, 2000, 2004, 8 golds, 3 silvers, 1 bronze), and Natalie Coughlin (2004, 2008, 2012, 3 golds, 4 silvers, 5 bronzes)

Dara Torres was 17 when she won her first medal at the 1984 Olympic Games in Los Angeles, swimming on a relay. She represented the United States on five Olympic teams (but she retired twice during her career, missing the 1996 and 2004 Games). At the 2000 Sydney Games, she was the oldest member of that team and earned five medals, more than any other swimmer at those Games. Eight years later, in the 2008 Games in Beijing, she won three more medals at the age of 42. In her last individual swim, the 50-meter freestyle, she lost the gold by a hundredth of a second to German swimmer Britta Steffen, 16 years her junior.

Americans Dara Torres, left, and Jenny Thompson, right, tied for bronze in the women's 100-meter freestyle, at the 2000 Olympic Games in Sydney.

Jenny Thompson was the mainstay for American swimming relays between 1992 and 2004, earning 10 medals for U.S. teams, swimming both freestyle and butterfly. At various times, she held world records in the 50- and 100-meter butterfly and 100-meter freestyle, as well as the 4x100-meter freestyle and medley relays. In world championship competition between 1997 and 2004, she earned 11 gold, 5 silver, and 2 bronze medals.

At the 2004 Games in Athens, U.S. swimmer Natalie Coughlin finished first in the women's 100-meter backstroke.

• STAT BOX •

Winning Big

Other U.S. female Olympic competitors who have won seven or more medals as of 2019:

- **Allyson Felix (track & field), 9**
- **Allison Schmitt (swimming), 8**
- **Shirley Babashoff (swimming), 8**
- **Dana Vollmer (swimming), 7**
- **Amanda Beard (swimming): 7**

Natalie Coughlin swims the women's 100-meter freestyle to win one of her six medals at the 2008 Olympic Games in Beijing.

At the 2000 Games in Sydney, Torres and Thompson actually tied for the bronze medal in the 100-meter freestyle.

Four years after winning five Olympic medals in the 2004 Olympic Games in Athens, Natalie Coughlin followed up that performance to become the first American woman to win six medals in a single Olympic Games—an accomplishment sadly overlooked in the shadow of Michael Phelps's eight gold medals in Beijing. She was the first woman to break the 60-second barrier in the 100-meter backstroke, and six years later she pushed the record below 59.00 seconds.

The most important thing in the Olympic Games is not to win but to take part, just as the most important thing in life is not the triumph but the struggle.

—Baron Pierre de Coubertin, 1894,
founder of the modern Olympic Games

POLITICS AND ENTERTAINMENT

Q: Which U.S. Olympians have appeared on the U.S. presidential ballots?

Hint:

As of 2019, none ran as either a Republican or a Democrat.

A: Benjamin Spock and Bob Richards

Benjamin Spock (rowing, 1924) was attending Yale in 1924 when he was placed on the U.S. men's eight rowing team that earned the gold medal in Paris. In 1946, after a successful career as a pediatrician, he authored *Dr. Spock's Baby and Child Care,* which was one of the top-selling books of the 20th century. His political activism led him to be placed on the 1972 U.S. presidential ballot as the candidate for the People's Party.

Bob Richards (track & field, 1948, 1952, 1956) won Olympic bronze and two gold medals in the pole vault and was a physical fitness pioneer, an ordained minister, and a popular motivational speaker with a religious fervor that led him to be called the "Vaulting Vicar." He was nominated by the Populist Party to run on the 1984 U.S. presidential ballot.

U.S. pole vaulter Bob Richards wins gold at the 1952 Games in Helsinki (left); at the 1924 Olympic Games in Paris, the champion crew team (below) includes future pediatrician Benjamin Spock, second from the coxswain.

Aiming for President

Bill Bradley was the youngest player on the gold-medal-winning 1964 U.S. Olympic basketball team before attending Oxford on a Rhodes scholarship. Later returning to basketball, he played 742 games for the New York Knicks, winning two NBA titles before winning one of New Jersey's Senate seats in 1977. After three terms as a U.S. senator, Bradley ran for the 2000 Democratic nomination, eventually losing that honor to the U.S. senator from Tennessee, Al Gore.

Helping the U.S. basketball team win gold at the 1964 Olympic Games, Bill Bradley later played professionally with the New York Knicks.

Q: Which film adaptation of an Olympian's life story won the Academy Award for the actor who played him?

Hint:

The movie does not mention the Olympic Games.

A: George Patton

A pentathlete on the 1912 U.S. Olympic team, George Patton later became a legend for his military service.

Recreational sports were late to arrive in many countries around the world, but almost every country supported a military presence. The modern pentathlon—a sport that requires running, swimming, fencing, shooting, and equestrian skills—was invented by Pierre de Coubertin for the Olympic Games as a way to draw more countries into the movement by appealing to their military officers.

George Patton attended the United States Military Academy at West Point, where he studied fencing and earned a spot on the 1912 U.S. Olympic team in the modern pentathlon competing at the Games in Stockholm. He finished fifth in the pentathlon but very likely would have earned a medal if not for his choice of weapon in the shooting event. The 26-year-old Patton was, by all accounts, an excellent shot owing to his military training. During the shooting competition, Patton fired 20 bullets at the paper target, but the event judges counted only 17 holes in the paper. Patton argued that he fired multiple rounds through some of the holes left by his earlier bullets and, because his .38-caliber weapon fired larger rounds than his competitors' .22-caliber weapons, the holes were larger than other shooters' and it was harder to distinguish individual entries. The judges found no evidence to prove his case and scored his round accordingly.

Patton finished 21st in the shooting portion, which may have cost him the chance to win any medal; still, he finished in a respectable fifth place overall. He was also selected for the 1916 Olympic team, but those Games were canceled because of World War I. Patton never competed in organized sports after the Stockholm Games; instead, he went on to a storied career in the armed forces.

Movie Legend

The 1970 film *Patton* tells the story of George Patton's military career, culminating with his leadership of the Allied forces invasion of Europe in World War II. The film earned 10 Academy Award nominations and won seven Oscars: Best Picture, Best Actor, Best Director, Best Story/Screenplay, Best Art Direction, Best Sound, and Best Film Editing. George C. Scott played the title role in an iconic fashion and earned the award for Best Actor, although he refused to accept the honor on philosophical grounds, saying actors' roles cannot be compared.

For his role as Gen. George Patton, actor George C. Scott won the Academy Award for Best Actor in 1970.

Q: Which Caucasian Olympic champion competing for the United States also raised his fist on the medal podium at the 1968 Olympic Games in Mexico City in solidarity with the American civil rights movement?

Unlike the African American track medalists Tommie Smith and John Carlos, he was neither reprimanded nor punished by the International Olympic Committee or U.S. Olympic team leaders.

A: Dick Fosbury

U.S. high jump gold medalist Dick Fosbury, on the medal podium at the 1968 Summer Games in Mexico City, raises his arm in support of civil rights.

Many Olympic fans recall Dick Fosbury because of his revolutionary backward style of clearing the high bar. In fact, the term "Fosbury Flop" was coined after a newspaper reporter compared Fosbury's style to a "fish flopping in a boat." Nevertheless, Fosbury won over the crowd and broke the Olympic record in Mexico City.

Fosbury was sympathetic to the civil rights movement, and in an attempt to show solidarity with African American sprinters Tommie Smith and John Carlos, who earlier had raised their fists in protest against the treatment of American blacks during the playing of the U.S. national anthem, he also raised his fist and lowered his head while standing on the gold-medal platform. The difference was that his gesture did not occur during the playing of "The Star Spangled Banner."

Fosbury was inducted into the U.S Olympic & Paralympic Hall of Fame in 1983, and Smith and Carlos were inducted in 2019.

I wanted to send a signal, a sign, that I was standing with all those fighting for Equal Rights.

—Dick Fosbury
(track & field, 1968, 1 gold medal)

Neutral Ground

According to IOC Olympic Charter, Rule 50, which was added in 2019, it now provides a framework to protect the neutrality of sport and the Olympic Games. It states that "No kind of demonstration or political, religious or racial propaganda is permitted in any Olympic sites, venues, or other areas."

At the 1968 Summer Games, U.S. sprinters Tommie Smith (center), who won gold, and bronze medalist John Carlos (right) raise their gloved fists to protest racism.

Q: Which Olympic champion has a star on the Hollywood Walk of Fame, which is also the *only* star to be hung on a wall instead of imbedded in the pavement?

Hint: The star was placed on the wall because the Olympian did not want anyone to step on the name.

A: Muhammad Ali

Under his birth name Cassius Clay, Muhammad Ali won the light heavyweight boxing gold medal at the 1960 Olympic Games in Rome, then immediately embarked on an illustrious professional career with more than 60 fights to his credit. Clay changed his name to Muhammad Ali after he joined the Nation of Islam in 1961. He was an outspoken opponent of the Vietnam War and a proponent of civil rights. He was also very entertaining, and his pre-fight prognostications were eminently quotable.

• STAT BOX •

In the Ring With Ali

Olympic boxers faced by Muhammad Ali during his professional career:

- Henry Cooper (1952, light heavyweight, Great Britain)
- Floyd Patterson (1952, middleweight, gold, U.S.A.)
- Joe Frazier (1964, heavyweight, gold, U.S.A.)
- Buster Mathis (1964, heavyweight until injured, U.S.A.)
- George Foreman (1968, heavyweight, gold, U.S.A.)
- Rudie Lubbers (1964, light heavyweight; 1968, heavyweight, Netherlands)
- Leon Spinks (1976, light heavyweight, gold, U.S.A.)
- Trevor Berbick (1976, heavyweight, Jamaica)

So many people tuned in for Ali's professional boxing bouts that the Hollywood Chamber of Commerce voted to consider boxing as "live performance" and to consider Ali's name for a star on the Walk of Fame. His star was approved in 2002. Ali asked that the star be mounted on the wall instead of laid into the cement walk because he felt it was wrong to allow people to walk on the name Ali shared with Muhammad, the Prophet of Islam.

Boxer Cassius Clay (top), later Muhammad Ali, trains for the 1960 Olympic Games. At right, on his 60th birthday Muhammad Ali gets a star on the Hollywood Walk of Fame.

Q: Which U.S. Olympic champion and U.S. Olympic & Paralympic Hall of Fame inductee became at 17 years of age the youngest and one of the first ever female sports reporters for a national television network?

She also led efforts to support Title IX opportunities for women in sport and chaired the 1999 FIFA Women's World Cup soccer championship, the most successful women's sporting event in history.

A: Donna de Varona

At 13, swimmer Donna de Varona was the youngest member of the 1960 U.S. Olympic team in Rome. While she was already the world record holder in the 400-meter individual medley, that event had not yet been included in the Olympic program, so she swam only in the preliminary heats of the 4x100-meter freestyle relay. The foursome that swam in the championship final (Joan Spillane, Shirley Stobs, Carolyn Wood, and Chris von Saltza) won the gold medal and broke the world record. Under current rules, de Varona would be entitled to a gold medal for her role in that event. During the next four years, de Varona established herself as one of the finest athletes in the world, winning two gold medals at the 1964 Games in Tokyo.

Donna de Varona retired from competitive swimming after winning two gold medals at age 17; she then became a sports commentator for ABC Sports.

Her post-athletic career began almost immediately after, when the 17-year-old was invited by ABC Sports president Roone Arledge to give reports on the network. She was instrumental in creating the 1978 Amateur Sports Act and the implementation of Title IX. She also chaired the 1999 FIFA Women's World Cup, which was the most watched women's sporting event in history: More than 90,000 people watched the final game of the tournament that generated a $4,000,000 profit and eventually led to the creation of the National Women's Soccer League.

Amateur Sports Act and Title IX

The 1978 Amateur Sports Act gave the U.S. Olympic Committee the power to charter national governing bodies for all Olympic sports and required significant athlete representation on all committees. The act was updated under the Ted Stevens Olympic and Amateur Sports Act in 1998, increasing athlete representation and granting the USOC monopoly status, Paralympian oversight, and protection from certain lawsuits. In 1972 Title IX prohibited institutions that received federal funding from discriminating on the basis of sex. This law was interpreted to provide increased scholarships and access to athletic programs for women, which led to a marked increase in female participation in Olympic sports.

Title IX allows women greater access to sport scholarships and athletic programs.

Q: At the 1976 Games in Montreal, women competitors were required to pass a gender test, and all but one were asked to submit a sample. Which female 1976 Olympian was exempted from this requirement?

Hint:

Her gender had already been publicly verified, and was far from suspect.

A: Princess Anne of Great Britain

The British royal family has a great deal of talent when it comes to horses, it seems. Her Royal Highness the Princess Anne, daughter of Queen Elizabeth, competed in three-day eventing equestrian competitions, earning medals at various European Eventing Championships. At the 1976 Olympic Games in Montreal, her husband was equestrian Mark Phillips, a gold medalist in the three-day team event at the 1972 Games and later a silver medalist at the 1988 Games in Seoul, South Korea. Their daughter, Zara, earned a silver on the British eventing team at the 2012 Olympic Games in London, and the medal was presented by her mother.

As the second child of Great Britain's Queen Elizabeth and Prince Philip, Princess Anne's genealogy was well documented, and her gender was never in question. Additionally, in equestrian events, athletes of both genders have competed against each other since 1964.

• STAT BOX •

Members of Royalty to Win Olympic Medals

- Crown Prince Olav V (sailing, 1928, gold, Norway)
- Constantine II (sailing, 1960, gold, Greece)
- Shaikh Ahmed Almaktoum (shooting, 2000, 2004 gold, 2008, United Arab Emirates)
- Princess Nathalie of Sayn-Wittgenstein-Berleburg (equestrian, 2008 bronze, 2012, Denmark)
- Prince Abdullah bin Mutaib Al Saud (equestrian, 2012, bronze, Saudi Arabia)
- Prince Friedrich Karl of Prussia (equestrian, 1912, bronze, Germany)
- Iñaki Urdangarín Liebaert (team handball, 1992, 1996, 2000 bronze, Spain)
- Count Hermann Alexandre de Pourtalès (sailing, 1900, silver and gold, Switzerland)

Obviously, it was amazing.

—Zara Phillips on receiving her medal from her mother

Britain's Princess Anne rides Goodwill (above) in the eventing competition at the 1976 Summer Games in Montreal. At the 2012 Games in London (right), Anne hugs her daughter, Zara Phillips, after presenting the silver medal to Zara's eventing team.

Q: In July 2011 two Olympians were joined in matrimony in one of the most heavily covered weddings of the year. Who were they?

Hint: The wedding was deemed a "royal wedding."

A: Albert Alexandre Louis Pierre Grimaldi (Albert II, prince of Monaco) and Charlene Wittstock of South Africa

More than a decade after meeting at a swim meet in Monte Carlo, Olympic bobsledder Prince Albert of Monaco and Olympic swimmer Charlene Wittstock of South Africa marry in 2011.

Grace Kelly was the daughter and sister of Olympic rowers, and also one of the top movie stars in the world when she left show business to marry Prince Rainier of Monaco. Their second child, Albert, grew into a competitive athlete, representing Monaco at five Olympic Winter Games in the sport of bobsled. He was appointed to the International Olympic Committee in 1985. He is the patron of the World Olympians Association and board member of the International Paralympic Committee (IPC).

In 2000, at a swim meet taking place in Monte Carlo, Albert met Charlene Lynette Wittstock, a Rhodesian-born member of the South African swimming team. Wittstock would later represent her country at the 2000 Olympic Games in Sydney, Australia, finishing fifth as a member of the 4x100-meter medley relay. The two were seen together at various Olympic-related events as early as 2006 and by 2010 had announced their engagement. The couple were married in July 2011, and the tabloids, which had been following this romance with great interest, gave the wedding wide coverage.

A Marriage of Medalists

In April 27, 1996, two very famous and popular Olympians were married in a state ceremony in an Orthodox church in Bucharest, Romania. Nadia Comaneci, the "Perfect 10" darling to the Romanian people, and her husband, Bart Conner, both champion gymnasts with 11 Olympic medals between them, were the guests of honor at a reception hosted by the country's president in the national White House. Conner and Comaneci, both in their mid-30s, invited 1,000 guests, and more than 10,000 well-wishers lined the streets for the occasion. The wedding was shown on live television in Romania, and highlights were played on ABC in the United States.

Romanian gymnast Nadia Comaneci marries American gymnast Bart Conner 20 years after scoring her perfect 10s at the 1976 Olympic Games in Montreal.

Q: Which feature film about the modern Olympic Games earned an Academy Award for Best Picture?

Hint:

Its producer was later killed in a car crash with a member of the British royal family.

A: Chariots of Fire

Runner Eric Liddell, nicknamed the "Flying Scotsman," won gold at the 1924 Olympic Games; the 1981 film *Chariots of Fire* tells his story.

Chariots of Fire, which depicted the lives of two British track stars at the 1924 Olympic Games in Paris, was nominated for seven Academy Awards and won four in 1981: Best Picture, Best Original Screenplay, Best Costume Design, and Best Original Score. The main characters, Eric Liddell and Harold Abrahams, were real Olympians who competed at the 1924 Olympic Games in Paris. Liddell was a devout Christian missionary and wanted to honor God through his running, and Abrahams was fighting against anti-Semitism.

Much of the plot, however, was slightly contrived to make for a more compelling story. In the movie, Liddell is depicted as dramatically deciding to drop out of Sunday's 100-meter heats for religious reasons after meeting team leaders on the ship; in fact, the decision to drop the 100-meter race and enter him in the 400-meter event was made before the ship left England. Also, Abrahams's victory in the 100-meter dash is shown as following his defeat in the 200-meter run, but in truth his winning race came before, not after, the 200-meter run event. Some other characters in the film are fictitious or come from different schools or periods. Nonetheless, the film was a great success and the music is iconic to this day.

Dodi Fayed, the son of Mohamed al-Fayed, the owner of Harrods, a popular British department store, was one of the producers of *Chariots of Fire* through his production company, Allied Stars. Other films he helped finance include *The World According to Garp,* starring Robin Williams, and Steven Spielberg's *Hook,* starring Julia Roberts. Fayed died in a car crash in Paris in 1997 while in the company of Diana, Princess of Wales.

• STAT BOX •

Hollywood and the Olympic Games

Many Hollywood films have ignited the athletic spirit with their portrayal of the Olympic Games. Below, those based on true stories indicate the Olympic year; the others are purely fictional.

- ***Cool Runnings*** **(bobsled, 1988)**
- ***Downhill Racer*** **(Alpine skiing, fictional)**
- ***Eddie the Eagle*** **(ski-jumping, 1988)**
- ***I, Tonya*** **(figure skating, 1994)**
- ***Jim Thorpe: All American*** **(track & field, 1912)**
- ***Miracle*** **(ice hockey, 1980)**
- ***Pentathlon*** **(modern pentathlon, fictional)**
- ***Personal Best*** **(track & field, fictional)**
- ***Race*** **(track & field, 1936)**
- ***Running Brave*** **(track & field, 1964)**
- ***Unbroken*** **(track & field, 1936)**

Q: Which Olympic champion twice successfully defended a title, winning three consecutive gold medals, then later earned a star on the Hollywood Walk of Fame?

Hint: The Walk of Fame star was not awarded for athletic prowess, but rather for a successful movie career.

A: Sonja Henie

Sonja Henie was born into an affluent Norwegian family in 1912, and at 11 years old she was competing on the ice in the 1924 Olympic Winter Games, where she finished eighth. Four years later she won her first of three gold medals in figure skating, which, as of 2020, makes her the most successful female figure skater of all time. On her way to 10 world championship titles, she is credited with being the first to incorporate artistic choreography and stylish costumes into her routines.

Henie's final Olympic appearance in 1936 was closely followed by her retirement from amateur sports, and she began appearing in figure skating exhibitions and professional ice shows around the United States. She was quickly signed by film producer Darryl Zanuck to a motion picture contract with Twentieth Century Fox, where she became one of the highest-paid female stars in the industry and appeared in a dozen films. In addition to receiving her star on the Hollywood Walk of Fame in 1960, she also has her hand and skate prints pressed into concrete at the TCL Chinese Theatre, formerly (but still colloquially) known as the Grauman's Chinese Theatre, in Hollywood, California.

Fifteen-year-old Sonja Henie of Norway won her first figure skating gold medal at the 1928 Games in Switzerland.

I want to do with skates what Fred Astaire is doing with dancing.

—Sonja Henie
(figure skating, 1924, 1928, 1932, 1936, 3 gold medals)

• STAT BOX •

Skating Champions

Other figure skaters who won multiple gold medals:

Men's singles:

- Gillis Grafström (1920 gold, 1924 gold, 1928 gold, 1932 silver, Sweden)
- Karl Schäfer (1932 gold, 1936 gold, Austria)
- Dick Button (1948 gold, 1952 gold, U.S.A.)
- Yuzuru Hanyu (2014 gold, 2018 gold, Japan)

Women's singles:

- Katarina Witt (1984 gold, 1988 gold, German Democratic Republic; 1994, Germany)

Pairs:

- Ludmila Belousova and Oleg Protopopov (1964 gold, 1968 gold, Soviet Union)
- Irina Rodnina and Alexander Zaitsev (1976 gold, 1980 gold, Soviet Union) (Rodnina also won gold in 1972 with a different partner.)
- Andrée Joly and Pierre Brunet (1924 bronze, 1928 gold, 1932 gold, France)

Ice Dance:

- Oksana Grishuk and Evgeni Platov (1994 gold, 1998 gold, Russia)
- Tessa Virtue and Scott Moir (2010 gold, 2014 silver, 2018 gold, Canada)

Q: Which two American Olympic champions are more famous for their movie acting careers than their athletic careers?

Hint:

They played the same fictional character but in different films.

A: Johnny Weissmuller and Buster Crabbe

In addition to winning 52 U.S. national championships and setting 51 world records, Johnny Weissmuller won five gold medals in swimming and a bronze in water polo across two Olympic Games (Paris in 1924 and Amsterdam in 1928). In 10 years of amateur swimming, Weissmuller won almost every race he ever entered, regardless of the stroke used. His fame and physique made him the ideal candidate for movie stardom, and he played Tarzan in 12 films between 1932 and 1948. He played the role of Jungle Jim in 13 films from 1948 to 1954 and in a 26-episode syndicated television series from 1955 to 1956.

A six-time Olympic medalist, U.S. swimmer Johnny Weismuller later starred in *Tarzan* films.

Following in Weissmuller's footsteps was another Olympic swimming champion, Clarence "Buster" Crabbe, who won a bronze in 1928 and a gold in 1932. A graduate of the University of Southern California, his good looks and swimming skill made him a natural choice to inherit the Tarzan role when he starred in *Tarzan the Fearless.* It was the first of his more than 100 films. In 1936 he starred as *Flash Gordon* in the first of three films in that franchise. Later, he landed the similar futuristic hero role of Buck Rogers in the 1939 film of the same name.

The Olympic gold medalist in 1932, U.S. swimmer Buster Crabbe went on to act in films, including *Flash Gordon*.

On the Big Screen

Olympians who have appeared in feature films, not playing themselves, include:

Alexi Pappas (track & field, 2016), *Olympic Dreams*

Bruce Jenner (track & field, 1972, 1976), *Can't Stop the Music*

Eleanor Holm (swimming 1932, 1936), *Tarzan's Revenge*

Glenn Morris (track & field, 1936), *Tarzan's Revenge*

Harold Sakata (weightlifting, 1948), *Goldfinger*

Herman Brix (track & field, 1928) (as Bruce Bennett), *Mildred Pierce, The Outsider*

Jim Thorpe (track & field, 1912), *Knute Rockne: All American*

Kurt Angle (wrestling, 1996), *Sharknado 2*

Mitch Gaylord (gymnastics, 1984), *Batman Forever*

Muhammad Ali (boxing, 1960), *Freedom Road*

Rafer Johnson (track & field, 1956, 1960), *License to Kill*

Shaquille O'Neal (basketball, 1996), *Kazam*

In the 1964 James Bond film *Goldfinger*, U.S. weightlifter and 1948 Olympic silver medalist Harold Sakata, left, played the villain Oddjob.

Q: Which Olympic champion's name appeared as the defendant in a case that was heard at the U.S. Supreme Court?

Hint: The Supreme Court sided with the Olympian, 8–0.

A: Boxer Cassius Clay, later known as Muhammad Ali

Former heavyweight champion Muhammad Ali in 1971, shortly after the Supreme Court overturned his conviction for draft evasion

After Cassius Clay won boxing's light heavyweight boxing gold medal at the 1960 Olympic Games in Rome, he immediately embarked on an illustrious professional career with more than 60 fights to his credit. In March 1964 he took the name Muhammad Ali. As the Vietnam War was escalating in 1966, Ali received notification that he was eligible for the U.S. Army draft, and he applied for conscientious objector status. His request was denied.

In April 1967 Ali didn't step forward when his name was called. As a result, the New York State Athletic Commission withdrew his boxing license, and the World Boxing Association stripped him of his professional heavyweight title. He was indicted by a federal grand jury and was convicted of violating Selective Service laws—a crime punishable by up to five years in jail plus a $10,000 fine. His plea to the Court of Appeals was denied.

Ali was not allowed a license to fight professionally from March 1967 to October 1970. During that time, the case eventually found its way to the U.S. Supreme Court and was argued in April 1971. Justice Thurgood Marshall recused himself because he had been the U.S. Solicitor General when the case was originally filed. On June 28, 1971, after serious deliberations, the court ruled 8–0 in favor of the defendant, mostly on procedural grounds and a technical error by the Justice Department.

Ali won his next 10 professional fights, six by knockouts, but he did not regain his world heavyweight title until he defeated the 1968 Olympic champion, George Foreman, in October 1974.

Ali's (Non-)Lucrative Years

On his way to the professional World Heavyweight Championship title in 1964, Ali went undefeated in 20 professional fights, including against Sonny Liston (right). Over the next two years, he established a boxing production company and won his next nine fights—five in 1966 alone. Having no boxing license from 1967 to 1970 prevented him from regaining his title when his ticket sales and television rights would have been record setting. Upon his return in 1970, his first attempt to reclaim the title, against Joe Frazier, earned the two boxers a combined $5 million purse. Between 1970 and 1978, Ali's earnings in the ring were estimated at $47.45 million. One can assume that he might have made twice that amount between 1967 and 1970.

Q: The 2010 book *Unbroken* and the 2014 movie of the same name tell the story of which Olympic runner?

Hint:

The majority of the film covers his exploits as a World War II survivor.

A: Louis Zamperini

After one tour as an Olympic athlete at the 1936 Games, U.S. runner Louis Zamperini served in World War II as a bombardier (inset).

At the 1936 Olympic Games in Berlin, American runner Louis Zamperini ran the last lap of the 5,000-meter race in 56 seconds, gaining some 45 meters on the leaders. Though his time of 14:46.8 did not earn him a medal, his flying finish thrilled the spectators and prompted a meeting with Adolph Hitler. While a student at the University of Southern California, it was predicted that he would be the first runner to cover a mile in less than four minutes, but his chances were reduced when World War II caused the next two Olympic Games to be canceled. Zamperini served in the South Pacific as a bombardier in the Army Air Corps.

On a reconnaissance run, Zamperini's plane crashed into the ocean. He survived on a raft for 47 days until he was captured by the Japanese and held as a prisoner of war for two and a half years. Upon returning home after the war, he suffered from post-traumatic stress disorder and nightmares of his treatment by a particularly brutal guard.

Zamperini's conversion at a revival by the evangelist Billy Graham brought an end to the nightmares and the beginning of his life of community service as a missionary. He also created a youth camp for juvenile delinquents. Zamperini was invited to carry the Olympic flame as part of the 1998 Nagano (Japan) Olympic Winter Games Torch Relay. The Louis Zamperini Lifetime Achievement Award is the highest honor that the U.S. Olympic and Paralympic Alumni can bestow.

• STAT BOX •

U.S. Champions in Distance Events

1,500 meters:
- James Lightbody (1904), 4:05.4, world record
- Mel Sheppard (1908), 4:03.4, Olympic record
- Matt Centrowitz, Jr. (2016), 3:50.00

5,000 meters:
- Bob Schul (1964), 13:48.8

10,000 meters:
- Billy Mills (1964), 28:24.4, Olympic record

3,000-meter steeplechase:
- Horace Ashenfelter (1952), 8:45.4, world record

Q: How many Olympic athletes have been invited to serve as grand marshal for the annual Tournament of Roses parade in Pasadena, California?

On multiple occasions, Olympians were selected as co-grand marshals.

A: Eight

Judo competitor Ben Nighthorse Campbell was the first Olympian so honored, appearing as co-grand marshal of the 1992 Rose Parade. He was not chosen for his athletic career as an Olympian in the 1964 Games, but rather for his role as a Native American who was also a U.S. senator. He shared the honor with a descendant of Christopher Columbus.

The year before the 1997 parade, two U.S. Olympic competitors had stood out at the 1996 Centennial Olympic Games in Atlanta, Georgia. Carl Lewis won his 10th Olympic medal and his fourth consecutive long jump gold, and Shannon Miller added two gymnastics gold medals to the five medals she had already won in Barcelona, Spain. They shared the 1997 parade honor.

In 2014 the 1936 Olympic runner Louis Zamperini received the invitation to be grand marshal because the tournament president admired the recently published book *Unbroken* about his Olympic experience and World War II survival. Sadly, Zamperini did not live to participate in the 2015 parade; his family rode down Pasadena's Colorado Boulevard in his place.

The city of Torrance's 2015 Rose Parade float was dedicated to Grand Marshal Louis Zamperini, who had passed away months before.

Co-grand marshals and Olympic champions diver Greg Louganis, sprinter Allyson Felix, and swimmer Janet Evans at the 128th Tournament of Roses parade in 2017

In 2016 Los Angeles celebrated receiving the honor of hosting the 2028 Olympic Games. Three Olympians and native Californians—diver Greg Louganis, swimmer Janet Evans, and sprinter Allyson Felix—had been instrumental in bringing the Games back to Los Angeles. All three served as co-grand marshals in 2017.

The 2020 Tournament of Roses parade president, Laura Farber, chose "The Power of Hope" as that year's theme, and she picked gymnast Laurie Hernandez as one of three women (and co-grand marshals) who exemplified the theme. In addition to her Olympic medals, Hernandez won the 2016 season of *Dancing With the Stars.*

• STAT BOX •

National Heroes

Many Olympians have been viewed as national heroes and are often invited to serve as featured guests on television shows and in parades. These Olympic athletes have appeared on the show *Dancing With the Stars* (as of 2019) and were declared the winners of their season. Many other Olympians and Paralympians have also competed on the program but did not win the Mirrorball Trophy.

- **May 2007: Apolo Ohno (short track speed skating, 2002, 2006, 2010)**
- **May 2008: Kristi Yamaguchi (figure skating, 1992)**
- **May 2009: Shawn Johnson (gymnastics, 2008)**
- **May 2014: Meryl Davis (figure skating, 2010, 2014)**
- **Nov. 2016: Laurie Hernandez (gymnastics, 2016)**
- **May 2018: Adam Rippon (figure skating, 2018)**

Olympic champions gymnast Shannon Miller and track & field star Carl Lewis as co-grand marshals of the 108th Rose Parade fulfill the 1997 parade's theme: "Life's Shining Moments."

As an HIV positive gay man and an Olympian, I felt the Rose Parade embodied the Olympic spirit of inclusion to welcome me, my husband and dog.

—**Greg Louganis** (diving, 1976, 1984, 1988, 4 gold medals, 1 silver)

THE GAMES

SUMMER, WINTER, AND PARALYMPIC

Q: In what sport can you win a *sprint* by moving as slowly as possible (occasionally almost staying perfectly still) *after* the start?

Hint:

Naturally, you must move eventually.

A: Track (velodrome) cycling

The match sprint is the shortest of cycling races around a banked velodrome track. Many riders prefer to draft off the leader, conserving strength for the ultimate sprint at the finish. If both riders choose the same tactics, they will often slow themselves to an almost stationary position, sometimes balancing in place, hoping to force their opponent into the lead. The standstill (called a track stand), might seem like a boring way to begin a race, but it actually increases the drama. Americans Mark Gorski and Nelson Vails met in the championship final of the 1984 Olympic Games in Los Angeles, and both tried to use a lesser version of that tactic. After two races, Gorski won gold and Vails took the silver medal. Gorski competed in 1984 and 1988. Vails, who began his cycling career as a bike messenger in New York City, became in 1984 the first African American cyclist to win an Olympic medal. He also appeared as a bicycle messenger in the film *Quicksilver.*

Mark Gorski, right, wins gold and Nelson Vails silver at the 1984 Olympic Games in Los Angeles.

When the match sprint was shortened from 1,000 meters to 750 meters in time for the 2000 Olympic Games, this balancing tactic became less significant, but many riders still ride very slowly for the first lap.

The track stand is like two gunslingers, staring at each other, waiting to be the second one to pull the trigger.

—Steve Hegg (cycling, 1984, 1 gold medal, 1 silver)

The Opposite of Sprint

In contrast to the sprint event is the road race. At the 1984 Olympic Games in Los Angeles, the women's road race made its debut, becoming the first ever Olympic cycling event for women. The course was five laps around an almost 16-kilometer (10 mi) loop. The 80-kilometer (50 mi) contest featured two Americans, Connie Carpenter-Phinney and Rebecca Twigg. Carpenter-Phinney had competed in speed skating at the 1972 Sapporo Olympic Winter Games and had since established herself as one of the top road cyclists in the world. Relative newcomer Twigg had beaten Carpenter-Phinney twice in the prior year. With 150 meters remaining, the lead pack had five riders, any one of whom might have won, but after more than two hours on the road, the two Americans delivered the strongest final push, and Carpenter-Phinney beat Twigg across the finish line by a single inch (below). Carpenter-Phinney retired shortly afterward, and Twigg went on to earn a bronze medal at the 1992 Games in Barcelona.

Q: In which two sports did Olympic athletes actually die during or as a direct result of Olympic competition?

Hint:

In both cases, hot weather contributed.

A: Cycling and road running

At the Games in Stockholm in 1912, Francisco Lázaro was Portugal's flag bearer as well as a competitor in the men's marathon. Around the 30.5-kilometer (19 mi) marker, he collapsed from what was thought to be heat stroke (his body temperature was measured at almost 106°F/41.1°C) and later died from what was diagnosed as "electrolyte imbalance." At the 1960 Games in Rome, Danish cyclist Knud Enemark Jensen was competing in the men's 100-kilometer team time trial (where three of the four entries must complete the course) when one of his teammates dropped out. When Jensen complained of light-headedness, his teammates naturally urged him to continue racing. When he finally collapsed, Jensen fell off his bicycle and hit his head on the pavement. He died without regaining consciousness. It was alleged that the Danish coach had administered a vasodilator prior to the accident. In part, because of this tragedy, the International Olympic Committee created a medical commission and instituted drug-testing beginning at the 1968 Games in Grenoble and Mexico City.

Danish cyclist Knud Enemark Jensen collapses from heat stroke during the 1960 Olympic Games in Rome; he will die a few hours later. An autopsy did not yield proof of any drugs in his system.

A memorial at the 2010 Winter Games in Vancouver, Canada, honors Georgian luger Nodar Kumaritashvili, who fatally crashed on a practice run.

Olympic Accidental Deaths

At the 1936 Games in Berlin, Romanian boxer Nicolae Berechet died three days after losing a bout in Olympic competition, but the reported cause of death was due to "blood poisoning." Also, various athletes have died as a result of training accidents at the Olympic sites. Most recently, at the 2010 Games in Vancouver, 21-year-old Georgian sledder Nodar Kumaritashvili crashed his luge on the final curve of a practice run and died at the hospital. His country created a postage stamp in his honor.

Q: USOP Hall of Fame inductees Jesse Owens and Al Oerter were each remarkable in their athletic accomplishments, but for different reasons. Carl Lewis (nicknamed "King Carl") was notable for doing both. What were these two different but equally remarkable accomplishments?

Hint: The same number is easily attached to each of these vastly different accomplishments.

A: Lewis earned four gold medals in a single Olympic Games, and he earned a gold medal in the same event in four consecutive Games.

U.S. runner Carl Lewis wins gold in the men's 100-meter sprint at the 1984 Olympic Games in Los Angeles.

Carl Lewis may rightly be remembered as the greatest track & field athlete of all time. His career Olympic medal total is nine golds and one silver over four Olympic Games. It might have been more if the United States had competed in the 1980 Games in Moscow because that year he won the NCAA title with a long jump that bettered the Olympic silver-medal-winning jump. Lewis was one of the stars of the 1984 Olympic Games in Los Angeles when he equaled Jesse Owens's 1936 record of four gold medals, winning in each of the same events. In 1988 he successfully defended his long jump title and finished second in the 200-meter race. Though he did not cross the finish line first in the 100-meter race in Seoul, he was awarded the gold medal after Canada's Ben Johnson was disqualified for drug use. In Barcelona he defeated the new long jump world record holder and 1988 silver medalist, Mike Powell, in a close contest. Ending his Olympic career in the same country where it began, Lewis's third jump at the Centennial Games in Atlanta was good enough (at 8.50 meters / 27 ft 10 ¼ in) to hold off the field and gave him his fourth gold medal in that event (tying Al Oerter's record for consecutive Olympic wins). Had Lewis been placed on the 1996 U.S. 4x100-meter relay, it is possible that he would have earned a 10th Olympic gold medal as well. In world championship competition, Lewis earned eight gold medals, a silver, and a bronze. He was voted "Sportsman of the Century" by the International Olympic Committee.

Jesse Owens and Al Oerter

Two record-setting Olympic champions in track & field paved the way for Carl Lewis's two remarkable accomplishments. Jesse Owens (right) won four gold medals at the 1936 Olympic Games in Berlin with wins in the 100-meters, 200-meters, long jump, and 4x100-meter relay. Al Oerter (left) won gold in the discus event in four consecutive Olympic Games, from 1956 through 1968.

Q: The United States boycotted the 1980 Olympic Games in Moscow, yet one American citizen was able to compete and win a medal at those Games. Who was it and how did they do it?

Hint: This athlete lived outside the United States at the time.

A: Mike Sylvester enjoyed dual citizenship with Italy and played on that nation's silver-medal-winning basketball team.

Sylvester played basketball at the University of Dayton, where in the 1974 NCAA championship tournament he scored 36 points against UCLA and legendary player Bill Walton, pushing the Bruins to triple overtime.

At the time, the Italian professional basketball league was looking to lure American players with Italian ancestry to play in Europe. Sylvester, a grandson of Italian immigrants, decided he was up for the challenge.

The six foot six inch (1.98 m) shooting guard made an impact almost immediately, helping his team from Milan win the 1975–76 FIBA European Cup Winners' Cup. In 1977 Sylvester was naturalized and was later traded to Pesaro, Italy, for an Italian record of $500,000. In 1980 he was invited to play on the Italian National Team, and his accurate shooting and playmaking earned his adopted country a spot in that year's Olympic basketball tournament.

Mike Sylvester receives his Olympic silver medal from an IOC member after playing for Italy in the 1980 Olympic Games in Moscow.

What Winners Get, and From Whom

Olympic medals are always presented to the winners by a member of the IOC. Accompanying the IOC member is a high-ranking official from the international federation that governs the sport. After the ceremony, each medalist is given a box or carrying case for their medallion and occasionally a diploma or certificate that documents their achievement.

Mike Sylvester shows off his framed medal and diploma from the 1980 Olympic Games.

When President Jimmy Carter called for an American boycott of the 1980 Games in Moscow, Sylvester's father contacted the U.S. Department of State for guidance and was advised the DOS would turn a blind eye to his decision. For Sylvester it was a simple choice, and the only one that would allow him to pursue his dream of becoming an Olympian.

At the Olympic Games, Italy upset the host country, 87–85, but lost to Yugoslavia in the gold-medal game, 86–77. With his team's silver, Italy won its first Olympic basketball medal, and Sylvester became the only American to medal at the 1980 Olympic Summer Games.

It was too incredible an opportunity. I had to take advantage of it.

—Mike Sylvester (basketball, 1980, 1 silver medal), on playing for Italy at the 1980 Olympic Games

Q: Who is the only Olympic champion to also win a Super Bowl ring?

Hint:

This athlete was so fast that some feel he forced the National Football League (NFL) to create the zone defense in order to restrain him.

A: Track & field star "Bullet Bob" Hayes

U.S. sprinter Bob Hayes won the gold medal in the 100-meter dash at the 1964 Olympic Games in Tokyo.

Bob Hayes attended Texas A&M University as both a runner and football player. He competed at the 1964 Games in Tokyo, where he was hand-timed at 9.9 seconds in the 100-meter sprint, becoming the first man to break the 10-second barrier. Sadly, rules at those Games required the automatic result to be listed as 10.0, which tied the world record and was two-tenths of a second faster than the silver medalist's time. Hayes accomplished the feat from lane one (badly worn from earlier, longer races) wearing borrowed shoes. Later, he anchored the U.S. 4x100-meter relay with a come-from-behind finish to earn a second gold medal. His split time (8.5–8.9, hand-timed) remains as of 2020 the fastest ever recorded in the event. Following his Olympic triumphs, Hayes left track to play football and was drafted as a wide receiver for the Dallas Cowboys. His transition was flawless; he gained over 1,000 yards in his first season and made 25 touchdowns in his first two seasons. He also set records for receiving and punt returns. He played in three Pro Bowls and, at the end of the 1971–72 season, he joined his Dallas teammates in Super Bowl VI in New Orleans with a 24–3 drubbing of the Miami Dolphins. Hayes was inducted into the Professional Football Hall of Fame in 2009.

• STAT BOX •

From the Games to the NFL

Several U.S. Olympians later became professional football players in the NFL.

- Bob Matthias (decathlon, 1948, 1952) (He was drafted but did not play.)
- Glenn Davis (track & field, 1956, 1960)
- Jim Thorpe (decathlon, pentathlon, 1912)
- Milt Campbell (decathlon, 1952, 1956)
- Ron Brown (track & field, 1984)
- Willie Gault (track & field, 1980; bobsled, 1988)

Running on the gridiron is very different from running on the track; similar, but very different.

—Willie Gault (bobsled, 1988, world record holder in 4x100-meter relay, NFL receiver 1983–1993)

Q: Which American high jumper tied the eventual 1956 Melbourne Olympic champion at 2.07 meters (6 ft 9 in) earlier that year, and also became a 1956 Olympic champion in a *different* sport?

Hint:

He is more famous for this other sport, and he was also presented the Presidential Medal of Freedom in 2011.

A: Bill Russell

Though his career in basketball is what Bill Russell will likely be remembered for, his athletic talents extend to track & field as well. In the high jump, he was ranked number seven in the world in 1956, and as a runner, he could cover 402 meters (440 yds) in less than 50 seconds. Drafted by the Boston Celtics, Russell postponed his professional career so that he could captain the 1956 U.S. Olympic basketball team, defeating the Soviets in the gold-medal game 89–55. President Barack Obama awarded Russell the Presidential Medal of Freedom at a ceremony in 2011.

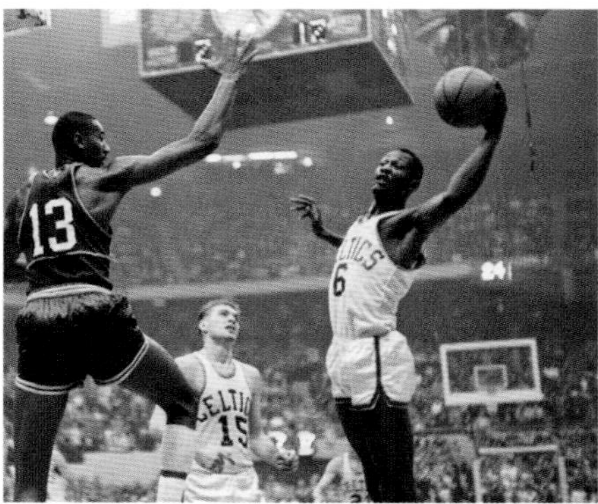

Going Pro

In professional basketball, Bill Russell (above, right) led the Boston Celtics to 11 national championships in 13 years. He was also the first African American to become the head coach in a major professional sport when he replaced Red Auerbach as the coach of the Celtics in April 1966.

Bill Russell, in USA shorts, helped the U.S. Olympic team win gold at the Olympic Games in Melbourne in 1956.

Q: Who is the *last* athlete to use the old "straddle" style in the high jump to win a gold medal at the Olympic Games?

Hint: This occurred long after Dick Fosbury retired from high jumping.

A: Christian Schenk

During the 1988 Olympic decathlon, East German Christian Schenk wins gold using the outdated straddle technique in the high jump instead of the Fosbury Flop.

This is a bit of a trick question. Following Dick Fosbury's victory in the high jump at the Mexico City Games in 1968, most of the world's high jumpers decided to abandon the old straddle style in favor of his revolutionary technique, the "Fosbury Flop." In fact, since the Mexico City Games, every men's Olympic high jump gold medal has been won by an athlete using Fosbury's technique. But in the decathlon competition, which includes the high jump in its 10 events, some athletes preferred to use the straddle style among the many diverse skills and strengths required. That was the case in 1988 when Christian Schenk from East Germany used the old technique in the high jump to clear the bar at 2.27 meters (7 ft 5½ in) on his way to an Olympic title and gold medal. The Olympic high jump event gold medal that year was awarded to the Ukrainian Gennadi Avdeenko, who cleared the bar at 2.38 meters (7 ft 9¾ in) and set a new Olympic record using the Fosbury Flop. Had Schenk competed in the high jump, his result would have placed him 13th.

A Winning Flopper

The first person to set a world record in the high jump using the Fosbury Flop was not Dick Fosbury, and it did not happen at the Olympic Games. Although Fosbury's flop of 2.25 meters (7 ft 4 in) in 1968 broke the Olympic record, he did not break the world record of 2.28 meters (7 ft 5 in) set by Valery Brumel in 1963. It was American Dwight Stones who did. In 1973 Stones "flopped" over the bar at 2.3 meters (7 ft 6 in) and set his first of three outdoor world records just one year after his bronze-medal performance at the 1972 Olympic Games. Stones was a deliberate technician, and he used both speed and spring to compete in three Olympic Games, earning two bronze medals. Afterward, Stones served as a television track & field analyst for decades.

In 1973 American Dwight Stones set a high jump world record in Munich using the Fosbury Flop.

Q: In 1904 Frank Kungler earned Olympic medals in three different sports, becoming the only person to do so in a single Olympic Games. What were the three sports?

Hint:

His body size and type was ideal for each sport, one of which is no longer on the Olympic program.

A: Wrestling, weightlifting, and tug-of-war

The 1904 Olympic Games in St. Louis, Missouri, were conducted in conjunction with the 1904 World's Fair. Events took place over the course of five months. Frank Kungler, a German immigrant who had settled in St. Louis, competed on the U.S. team. He may have been small (5 ft 6½ in, 165 lb/1.69 m, 74.8 kg), but he was among the strongest men to compete: He earned two bronze medals in weightlifting (in the single two-handed lift and the nine-event dumbbells competition) while also earning a bronze medal as a member of an American tug-of-war team. His best result, however, was a silver medal as a heavyweight wrestler. While Kungler did not become a U.S. citizen until 1913, the International Olympic Committee considers his performances at the 1904 Olympic Games as representing the United States.

• STAT BOX •

Off the Roster

Besides tug-of-war, other discontinued Olympic sports include the following:

- Alpinism (speed climbing up the Alps)
- Cricket
- Croquet
- Jeu de paume (precursor to tennis)
- Field handball (outdoors, 11 to a side)
- Lacrosse
- Military patrol (combination of biathlon and ski-mountaineering)
- Motor boating
- Pelota (a court sport played with ball and hand)
- Polo
- Rackets (similar to squash)
- Roque (similar to croquet)

At the 1904 Olympic Games in St. Louis, held concurrently with the World's Fair, Frank Kungler and his St. Louis team take on the New York Athletic Club in a tug-of-war. They later win an Olympic bronze medal for the event.

Q: What Olympic medal-winning feat did swimmer Ryan Lochte accomplish *twice* that neither Michael Phelps nor Mark Spitz ever attempted?

Hint:

Amazing as it was, it was a matter of luck rather than choice.

A: He won two individual (not relay) event medals on the same day.

U.S. swimmer Ryan Lochte shows his gold medal for the men's 200-meter backstroke at the 2008 Olympic Games in Beijing.

Each day's Olympic swim schedule usually offers gold-medal racing in two men's events, two women's events, and one relay. The schedulers avoid difficult "doubles" (where a swimmer must race in two championship finals on the same day). For example, Games organizers won't offer both backstrokes or two distance races for the same gender on the same day. Additionally, butterfly and freestyle are so similar that those strokes are usually placed on separate days. Fortunately for Michael Phelps and Mark Spitz, each of their individual races at the Olympic Games occurred on different days. Though Lochte raced against Phelps in the 200-meter and 400-meter individual medleys and with him on various relays, Lochte also competed in the 200-meter backstroke, an event that often occurs on the same day as the 200-meter I.M. At the 2008 Olympic Games in Beijing, while all eyes were focused on Michael Phelps's attempt to win eight gold medals, Lochte elected to swim the double (200-meter backstroke and 200-meter I.M.) knowing that his chances against Phelps in the I.M. would be hurt by his racing the backstroke. On August 15, Lochte won the 200-meter backstroke, and 27 minutes later raced in the 200-meter I.M., finishing third behind Phelps by 2.3 seconds. Four years later Lochte attempted it again at the Games in London: He earned a bronze in the 200-meter backstroke half an hour before he won a silver in the 200-meter I.M., 0.63 seconds behind Phelps. As of 2019, the versatile Lochte is the proud winner of 12 Olympic medals, six of them gold.

Difficult Double Feats

The first Olympic double in swimming occurred on July 19, 1976, at the Games in Montreal, when I earned a silver medal in the 200-meter freestyle, just 45 minutes after I won gold in the 100-meter backstroke. But perhaps the most unbelievable double occurred three days later on July 22, when East German Kornelia Ender (left) swam the 100-meter butterfly final and minutes later also swam the 200-meter freestyle final, winning both races with comfortable margins. However, her Olympic results have been disputed for years because it was later discovered that the East German sports program had been systematically doping their athletes, giving them an unfair advantage.

Q: Who was the last American athlete to compete at the Olympic Games while simultaneously serving as an expert analyst for the national television coverage?

Hint:

This double-medal-winning athlete almost won a third medal at these Games while also doing "double duty."

A: Dwight Stones

Sports Illustrated referred to high jumper Dwight Stones as "The Mouth That Soars" because of his easy command of the English language, his world record heights achieved, and his frequent use of long, run-on sentences. After winning bronze medals at the 1972 and 1976 Olympic Games, he became a vocal proponent for allowing athletes to receive financial compensation. His acceptance of prize money from the ABC *Superstars* (a televised reality sports competition) resulted in a 17-month suspension from competition. After returning to his sport, he was invited to share his opinions at various track & field competitions, and he developed into an accomplished sports announcer and reporter. After almost eight years without a personal best jumping result, Stones agreed to work on the Olympic broadcast for ABC Sports. Without high expectations, he tried out for the 1984 U.S. Olympic team and surprisingly set a new American record. In the Olympic Village, Stones was given two credentials (media and athlete). Stones had to schedule his time wisely if his on-camera work and sport were to coexist, but he made himself available to report on all the Olympic track & field events except the men's high jump. He didn't win a medal in Los Angeles, but his fourth-place performance was almost 10 centimeters (4 inches) higher than his medal-winning heights in prior Games. After discovering that a competitor had simultaneously been a broadcast journalist, the International Olympic Committee insisted that henceforth only one credential would be permitted per person.

After setting a new high jump American record in the trials, Dwight Stones finishes fourth in the 1984 Olympic Games in Los Angeles.

Once a Swimmer, Always a Swimmer

At the 1990 U.S. Short Course Swimming National Championships in Nashville, Tennessee, I was working as the play-by-play announcer for Turner Broadcasting with expert analyst Rowdy Gaines, the swimming triple-gold medalist from the 1984 Games (left). Before the consolation finals of the 50-yard freestyle, Rowdy took off his headphones and ran down to the pool deck. The 31-year-old swimmer jumped onto the starting blocks and dove into the water, racing against swimmers much younger than himself. He did not win the race, but he did set a new masters record for the 30–34 year age group. Moments later, wrapped in a beach towel, Gaines returned to the booth with hair still wet and continued his commentary.

Q: When Olivér Halassy represented Hungary in three Olympic Games, he competed with only one foot. He also earned two gold medals and one silver. In what sport did he compete?

Hint: His medals came in a team sport.

A: Water polo

At the age of 11, Olivér Halassy lost his left leg below the knee when he was hit by a street car. This didn't stop him from becoming a competitive swimmer who earned 25 national swimming titles and the 1931 European Championship in the 1,500-meter swim. Compared to water polo players, long-distance swimmers do not need to kick very hard, and Halassy did not use a prosthetic. A popular and natural leader, he played water polo for Hungary at the 1928, 1932, and 1936 Olympic tournaments, playing in every game (earning silver in 1928 and gold in both 1932 and 1936). He scored 20 goals in Olympic competition. He was killed in what is believed to be a robbery attempt in 1946, three days before his wife gave birth to their third child.

Despite losing a leg as a child, Hungary's Olivér Halassy swam competitively and played water polo in three Olympic Games, winning two gold medals and a silver.

"Blood in the Water" Game

The 1956 Games in Melbourne, Australia, took place just weeks after Soviet tanks had rolled into Hungary in an effort to suppress a revolt against Communist rule. When the Soviet water polo team faced Hungary's team in the semifinals, some hostility was expected. The match was very physical, with many punches and kicks by players on both sides. Hungary was leading 4–0 when, during a break in the action, Soviet Valentin Prokopov landed his fist above Ervin Zádor's right eye, which began to bleed profusely (right). Officials stopped the competition, which was later known as the "blood in the water" game. The win was awarded to Hungary, which went on to defeat Yugoslavia in the gold-medal game. Half the Hungarian Olympic delegation did not return to Hungary after the Games.

Q: Who is the only athlete to win an Olympic gold medal in five consecutive Games?

Hint: Though the accomplishment was in one sport, it involved three different events.

A: Sir Steve Redgrave

A member of the British Olympic rowing team, Steve Redgrave was knighted by the Queen of England on May 1, 2001, for his excellence and longevity in the sport. His winning streak began at the 1984 Games in Los Angeles, where he struck gold in the coxed four event. At the 1988 Games in Seoul he won gold in the coxless pair event (he also won a bronze in the men's coxed pairs), and again in Barcelona in 1992 and Atlanta in 1996, also for the coxless pairs events. He was selected as the British Olympic team Opening Ceremony flag bearer at both the 1992 and 1996 Games. After returning from a short self-imposed retirement, he won gold again at the 2000 Games in Sydney, competing in the coxless four event. He had been diagnosed with colitis in 1992 and diabetes in 1997, yet he was still able to accomplish his results in spite of the symptoms and treatment for the diseases.

• STAT BOX •

Rowing Terms

There are 14 Olympic rowing events scheduled for the 2021 Olympic Games, seven each for both men and women. Sculling athletes pull on two oars each, while rowers in the other events use one oar apiece, in a motion called sweep. A boat carrying a coxswain to steer and coach is coxed; without a coxswain, it is coxless.

- Single sculls
- Double sculls
- Lightweight double sculls
- Quadruple sculls
- Coxless pairs
- Coxless fours
- Coxed eight

Britain's Steve Redgrave (left) and Andy Holmes on their way to winning gold in the men's coxless pairs at the 1988 Olympic Games

Q: When Bob Beamon delivered the "leap into the 21st century" at the 1968 Mexico City Games, shattering the long jump world record by almost 0.6 meters (2 ft), whose American record did he break?

Hint: The owner of this record, set in 1960, bettered the record of the legendary Jesse Owens, set in 1935.

A: Ralph Boston

American Ralph Boston first breaks the long jump world record in 1960, and goes on to break it five more times between 1960 and 1965.

Jesse Owens had set the long jump world record at a meet in Michigan in 1935, landing in the pit at 8.13 meters (26 ft 8 ¾ in). Ralph Boston broke that mark in 1960, with a jump of 8.21 meters (26 ft 11¼ in). He then proceeded to break the world record in the long jump an amazing six times between 1960 and 1965, winning Olympic gold in 1960 and silver in 1964. In 1965 Boston's best stood at 8.35 meters (27 ft 4¾ in). In 1967 Boston began unofficially coaching Bob Beamon, and then he watched his pupil demolish his own world record by nearly 0.6 meters (2 ft) at the 1968 Games in Mexico City. At the same Games, Boston won the bronze after qualifying first with a distance of 8.03 meters (26 ft 4⅛ in), which would have won the silver had he done it in the final. Boston and Beamon both retired from competition shortly thereafter. In 1983 Beamon was a member of the first class of U.S. Olympic and Paralympic Hall of Fame inductees, and Boston was inducted two years later.

Somersault Technique

During the 1970s some athletes were experimenting with a new way to do the long jump. They found that a forward somersault in the middle of the jump would provide more forward rotation and less drag than the conventional method. While competing for Washington State University, New Zealand's Tuariki Delamere brought more attention to the technique when he tied the 1972 Olympic champion, Randy Williams, in a conference meet, clearing 7.79 meters (25 ft 6¾ in). The method was being tried by various international jumpers, and by America's future decathlon champion, Bruce Jenner, as well. In 1975, citing safety concerns, the International Association of Athletics Federations banned the somersault from use in long jump competitions, so Delamere will forever be the record holder in the long jump with that technique.

A somersault performed in the middle of a long jump helped some athletes in the 1970s to jump farther.

Q: John Wooden, who coached basketball at UCLA from 1948 to 1975, was one of the greatest coaches of all time, and yet only two of his UCLA Bruin players participated in the Olympic Games. Who were they?

Hint: One of them participated in a sport other than basketball in the Games.

A: Rafer Johnson and Walt Hazzard

By the time Rafer Johnson graduated from UCLA and John Wooden's Bruin varsity basketball team in 1959, he had already made quite a name for himself: a world record breaker, *Sports Illustrated* Sportsman of the Year, Sullivan Award as the nation's outstanding amateur athlete, 1956 Olympic silver medalist, and UCLA student body president. Wooden said Johnson was "one of the finest persons" he had ever known. But Johnson's first love was track & field, not basketball. In 1960 Johnson was chosen to be the U.S. Olympic team's flag bearer and went on to win the decathlon gold medal.

The U.S. basketball team stands on top of the medal podium at the 1964 Olympic Games in Tokyo. The Soviets won the silver and Brazil took bronze.

U.S. decathlete Rafer Johnson won gold in the 1960 Olympic Games.

Two years later, Walt Hazzard was a member of Wooden's first Bruin team to compete in the National Collegiate Athletic Association (NCAA) Final Four—the nationwide basketball playoffs. In 1964 Hazzard was voted most valuable player (MVP) of the first national title-winning team at UCLA; he also led the U.S. Olympic basketball team to win the gold medal at the 1964 Games in Tokyo.

Non-Olympic Stars

Neither of Wooden's two best players became Olympians. Karem Abdul-Jabbar (born Ferdinand Lewis Alcindor) was not on the 1968 team because he didn't feel like helping a country that denied some people their civil rights. Bill Walton was willing to play for the United States but was unwilling to go through repeated tryouts and participate in what he called "endless exhibitions." Both players had successful professional careers.

UCLA coach John Wooden with star basketball player Lew Alcindor at the 1969 NCAA championship finals in Louisville, Kentucky

Q: In what Olympic track & field event does the official International Olympic Committee (IOC) record not show an Olympic champion?

Hint: The official record shows two silver medalists, with different results.

Uh-Oh!

A: Women's 100-meter dash at the 2000 Games

The big star at the track in the 2000 Games in Sydney, Australia, was American runner Marion Jones, who received five medals: two bronzes and three golds, including one gold for the 100-meter dash. Seven years later, Jones admitted to using performance-enhancing drugs (PEDs) prior to the 2000 and 2004 Games, and the IOC immediately stripped her of all her medals. The runner-up in the 100-meter sprint in Sydney was Ekaterini Thanou from Greece. Normally, she would have been promoted to the gold medal but, at the time of Jones's revelations, Thanou had also been implicated in a possible PED scandal. The suspicions without proof were not enough to disqualify her 2000 result, but the IOC elected to deny her the gold medal anyway. Two Jamaicans, Tanya Lawrence and Merlene Ottey, were elevated to second and third place, respectively. As of 2020 the gold medal spot remains vacant in the official Olympic results.

U.S. runner Marion Jones crosses the finish line ahead of Greece's Ekaterini Thanou in the women's 100-meter dash at the 2000 Olympic Games in Sydney.

Sweden's Anders Ahlgren and Finland's Ivar Böhling grapple at the 1912 Games in Stockholm.

Wrestling Tie

At the 1912 Games in Stockholm, the Olympic rules of Greco-Roman wrestling required the champion to actually defeat his opponent. When Anders Ahlgren of Sweden and Ivar Böhling of Finland met in the final, the two men were so evenly matched that neither competitor would concede defeat. The two men struggled against each other for nine hours before the judges lost patience. Eventually, the officials decided to grant both athletes a silver medal. No winner was declared.

When a cheater wins it denies an athlete the immediate gratification of receiving their medals but far worse, it denies their Olympic legacy forever!

—Wendy Boglioli
(swimming, 1976, 1 gold medal, 1 silver, 1 bronze)

Q: Swimmer Michael Phelps holds the record for most gold medals won in a single Olympic Games, winning eight in 2008. Swimmer Mark Spitz had the previous record with seven. Two other Olympians have each earned six gold medals in a single Games. Who are either of these champions?

Hint: Their sports were swimming and gymnastics.

A: Swimmer Kristin Otto and gymnast Vitaly Sherbo

German swimmer Kristin Otto (top) won six gold medals at the 1988 Games in Seoul. In Barcelona four years later, gymnast Vitaly Scherbo (above) of Belarus matched her result.

At the 1988 Olympic Games, the winningest athlete was Kristin Otto from East Germany. Otto was tall (6 ft 1 in/1.85 m) and imposing. She had earned four gold and two silver medals at the 1986 world championships, swimming freestyle, backstroke, and butterfly. The East German women also had great relay teams. In Seoul Otto was the one really cleaning up in the pool, winning individual gold medals in the 50-meter freestyle (newly added), 100-meter freestyle, 100-meter butterfly, and 100-meter backstroke, as well as two team golds for the 4x100-meter freestyle and 4x100-meter medley relays. Otto retired from competition in 1989 and became a television sports reporter.

At the 1992 Games, a 20-year-old from Belarus, Vitaly Sherbo, was the master of the gymnasium. Sherbo had arrived on the gymnastics scene in 1991 with a perfect 10.0 vault at the European championships and the all-around silver medal at the world championships. In Barcelona he earned five individual gold medals (all-around, pommel horse, still rings, vault, and parallel bars) and one more as a member of the Unified Team. Sherbo successfully defended his all-around title at the 1993 world championships.

Despite personal issues (he was burglarized and his wife was injured in a car accident), he was still able to win four more medals (all bronze) at the 1996 Games in Atlanta. Sherbo now owns a school of gymnastics in Las Vegas, Nevada.

• STAT BOX •

Five-Gold Winners

As of 2020, winning five *individual* gold medals (not relay or team events) in a single Olympic Games is something only achieved by Vitaly Sherbo and two other athletes:

- **1980: Eric Heiden (speed skating)**
- **2008: Michael Phelps (swimming)**

PED Doubts

Kristin Otto's results at the 1988 Games (left) may have been overlooked on the global stage because of suspicions surrounding the possible use of banned substances. In fact, proof was discovered in 1991 that the East German sports medicine doctors had been supplying their athletes with PEDs, which cast doubt on all of the team's results. Some of Otto's teammates admitted to the cheating, but Otto claimed she was never aware of any wrongdoing.

Q: Which American Olympic *decathlon* champion is also represented in the International Swimming Hall of Fame?

Hint:

He was inducted after receiving the Gold Medallion, the International Swimming Hall of Fame's highest honor.

A: Milt Campbell

American Milt Campbell, center, in the 110-meter hurdles event, finished second in the decathlon at the 1952 Games in Helsinki; at the 1956 Games in Melbourne, he won gold and set a new Olympic record.

In high school Campbell excelled in football, wrestling, and track. In an era when African Americans were not expected to excel at swimming, he also earned all-state honors in the water. His coach told him that the only way he could be declared the best athlete in the world was to win the Olympic decathlon title. At the 1952 Olympic Games he won the decathlon silver medal and four years later he returned to break the Olympic record and win gold, defeating world record holder Rafer Johnson in the process. Campbell's result in the hurdles portion of the decathlon would have earned a bronze medal in the 110-meter hurdles event at the same Games. In 1989 Campbell was inducted into the National Track & Field Hall of Fame and 23 years later, he was presented the Golden Medallion award by the International Swimming Hall of Fame for his multiple athletic talents and his role in inspiring youth. In receiving this award, he joined such luminaries as Art Linkletter, Esther Williams, and Ronald Reagan. Campbell became the first and, as of 2020, the only person inducted into *both* the National Track & Field and International Swimming Halls of Fame.

• STAT BOX •

Decathlon Golds

U.S. Olympic decathlon champions:

- Jim Thorpe (1912)
- Harold Osborn (1924)
- Jim Bausch (1932)
- Glenn Morris (1936)
- Bob Mathias (1948, 1952)
- Milt Campbell (1956)
- Rafer Johnson (1960)
- Bill Toomey (1968)
- Bruce Jenner (1976)
- Dan O'Brien (1996)
- Bryan Clay (2008)
- Ashton Eaton (2012, 2016)

Whenever someone has told me that I can't do something, it has become my mission in life to prove them wrong.

—Milt Campbell (track & field, 1952,1956, 1 gold medal, 1 silver)

Q: Why did two Olympic medalists have their medals cut in half?

They competed against each other.

A: Their friendship mattered more than their placings in the 1936 men's pole vault event.

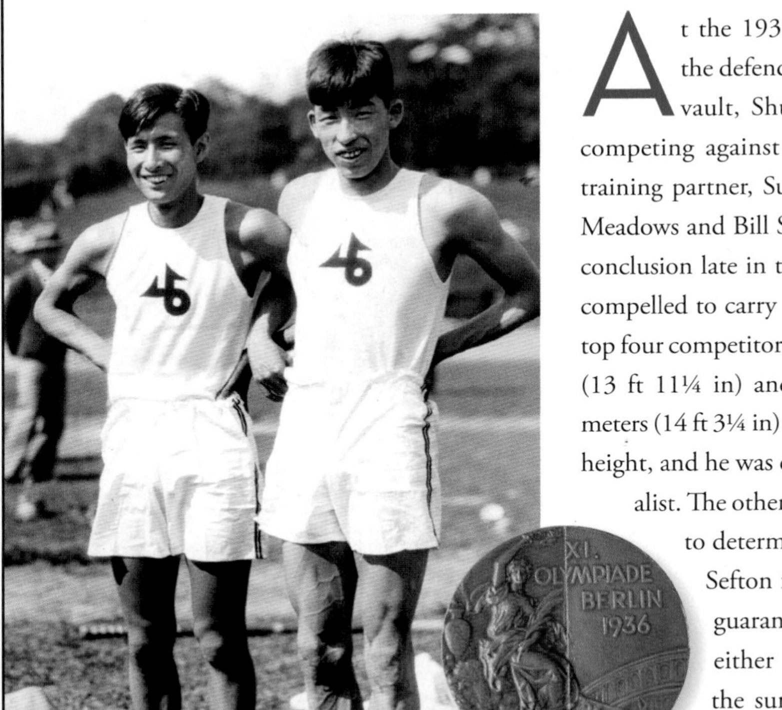

Japanese pole vaulters and friends, Shuhei Nishida, right, and Sueo Oe cut and fused their silver and bronze medals from the 1936 Olympic Games in Berlin.

At the 1936 Olympic Games in Berlin, the defending silver medalist in the pole vault, Shuhei Nishida, found himself competing against his Japanese teammate and training partner, Sueo Oe, and Americans Earle Meadows and Bill Sefton. As the event drew to a conclusion late in the evening, the jumpers were compelled to carry on under artificial lights. The top four competitors cleared the bar at 4.25 meters (13 ft 11¼ in) and the bar was raised to 4.35 meters (14 ft 3¼ in). Only Meadows cleared at that height, and he was declared the event's gold medalist. The other three vaulters held a jump-off to determine the remaining places, and Sefton failed to clear the first height, guaranteeing both Japanese athletes either a silver or bronze medal. To the surprise of the officials, neither Oe nor Nishida wanted to keep competing against each other, and the Japanese delegation was given the responsibility of deciding which medal to award each competitor. Nishida was chosen as the silver medalist and Oe received the bronze.

When the two teammates returned to Japan, they had a jeweler cut their medals in half; one half of each medal was fused to the corresponding half of the other. These two unique medals are now referred to as the Friendship Medals.

Medal Decision

Currently, if jumpers tie during the Games, the medals are decided on the basis of which jumper had the fewer misses at the earlier heights. These rules were not in effect in 1936; however, it was on this basis that Shuhei Nishida was chosen by his nation as the silver medalist.

Q: In what Olympic event was there a four-way tie for a medal?

Hint: It happened on American soil and involved an American.

A: Gymnastics (men's vault, 1984)

At the 1984 Olympic Games in Los Angeles, Chinese gymnast Lou Yun wins gold, while silver is shared by four competitors, including American Mitch Gaylord (in blue).

UCLA's Pauley Pavilion was the site of Coach John Wooden's basketball dynasty, and at the 1984 Olympic Games in Los Angeles it was also the site of gymnastics competition. In a thrilling team battle, the men of the United States pulled off a great upset by defeating the teams from Japan and China.

The individual performance scores in the team battle were carried over to determine the finalists in each of the individual events. Half the total would be added to a final performance score on the individual apparatus.

In the team competition, China's Lou Yun dominated with a perfect 10.0 on both of his vaults. He carried that score into the finals, where he added an almost perfect 9.950 to win the gold medal with a total of 19.950 out of a possible 20 points. The fight for the silver medal was much closer as two athletes from Japan, one from China, and one from the United States all tied with a score of 19.825. When the medals were presented, Lou got the gold, and silver medals were presented to Li Ning (China), Koji Gushiken (Japan), Mitch Gaylord (U.S.A.), and Shinji Morisue (Japan). As of 2020, it was the only time in Olympic history when four individuals shared the same step on the medal podium in an individual event.

Packed Podium

The most crowded Olympic medal podium occurred at the 1980 Olympic Winter Games in Lake Placid. U.S. hockey team captain Mike Eruzione, designated to represent the team for the playing of the national anthem, stood alone on the small podium where earlier the athletes had individually stood to receive their gold medals. Immediately afterward, he beckoned his 20 teammates (right) to join him on the podium in celebration. Eruzione said the entire group had to cling to each other, "jostling for position like worker bees," to prevent anyone from falling off.

Q: In what sport did an American athlete win six Olympic medals on the same day?

Hint:

This athlete also had a wooden leg.

A: Gymnastics

The 1904 Olympic Games were conducted in conjunction with the World's Fair in St. Louis, Missouri, and the various events were spread out over the course of several months. In gymnastics, the all-around and team events and the gymnastics triathlon (an event soon discontinued) took place in July, while the other eight individual apparatus events took place in October. A local gymnast, George Eyser, had been training for these Games. In his youth he had lost his left leg after it was run over by a train, but he was able to train and compete with a wooden prosthetic. On October 29, 1904, the 34-year-old Eyser, who had not competed in July, won Olympic gold medals in the vault, parallel bars, and rope climb events; silver medals in the pommel horse and combined (a combination of the parallel bars, horizontal bar, vault, and pommel horse) events; and a bronze medal in the horizontal bar event. His teammate Anton Heida also won six medals in those Games (five gold and one silver), but his team gold medal had been earned in July.

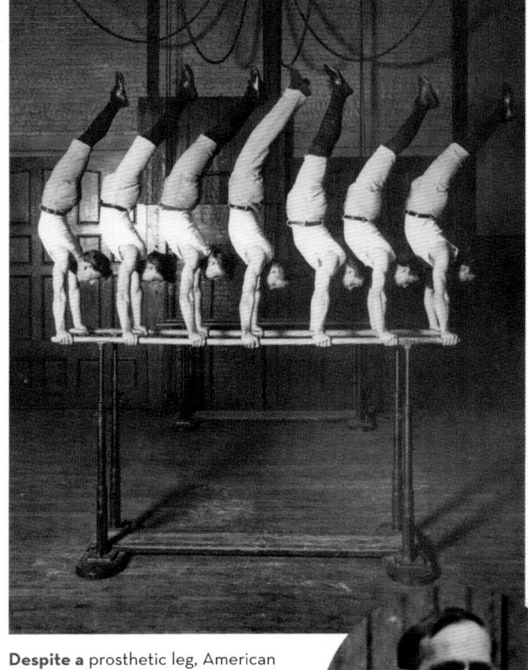

Despite a prosthetic leg, American gymnast George Eyser (right, and center with his team above) won three gold medals, two silvers, and a bronze at the 1904 Olympic Games in St. Louis, on the same day.

• STAT BOX •

Persevering Champions

Some athletes who did not have all their limbs while competing in the Olympic Games:

- **Olivér Halassy (water polo, 1928, 1932, 1936, Hungary): Lost left leg in a street car accident.**
- **Károly Takács (shooting, 1948, 1952, Hungary): Lost right hand to a faulty grenade.**
- **Natalie du Toit (swimming, 2008, South Africa): Lost left leg in a car accident.**
- **Oscar Pistorius (track & field, 2012, South Africa): Both feet amputated because of a congenital defect.**
- **Natalia Partyka (table tennis, 2012, Poland): Born without right hand and forearm.**

More amazing than his six medals in a single day might be his ability to win the gold medal in the vault...on one leg! Eyser is a true champion!

—Peter Vidmar (gymnastics, 1984, 2 gold medals, 1 silver)

Q: U.S. athlete Sheila Taormina qualified for four consecutive Olympic teams, participating in a total of three different summer sports. What were her three sports?

Hint:

An element of her first sport was involved in each of her subsequent sports.

A: Swimming, triathlon, and modern pentathlon

Sheila Taormina shows off her 1996 gold medal in swimming.

As a swimmer, Sheila Taormina earned a gold medal competing in the 4x200-meter relay at the 1996 Centennial Games in Atlanta, and she was the only American swimmer to compete in both the heats and final of that relay. Following her Atlanta success, she turned her attention to the newest sport added to the 2000 Olympic program, the triathlon (swimming, cycling, and running). She qualified to represent the United States at the 2000 Games in Sydney, Australia, where she finished sixth, and the 2004 Games in Athens, Greece, where she finished 23rd. Her Olympic hunger was not yet satisfied, so she took up the modern pentathlon (fencing, shooting, swimming, horsemanship, and running) and earned a spot on the 2008 U.S. Olympic team. She competed in Beijing, China, finishing 19th. The element that these sports have in common is water.

Athletes for All Seasons

As of 2020, only two athletes have been declared the champion in both winter and summer Olympic or Paralympic competition. American Eddie Eagan won gold in boxing for the lightweight class in the 1920 Olympic Games in Antwerp and for the four-man bobsled in the 1932 Games in Lake Placid. And five-time Paralympian Alana Nichols won gold in wheelchair basketball in 2008 (Beijing) and in downhill and giant slalom skiing in 2010 (Vancouver), and a silver in the downhill in 2014 (Sochi).

America's Eddie Eagan, right, won gold for boxing in 1920, and for bobsled in 1932.

I have a funny little skill for learning new things and understanding what goes into the making of something.

—Sheila Taormina (swimming, 1996, 1 gold medal; triathlon, 2000, 2004; pentathlon, 2008)

Q: The shortest-lasting world record was set at the Olympic Games. In what sport/event was this record set?

Hint:

The record lasted for 1.14 seconds.

A: Women's pentathlon

The pentathlon is a five-event competition (similar to the 10-event decathlon) where points are awarded in each event based on the objective measurement of performance. At the start of the 1972 Games in Munich, Germany, the world record of 4,775 points had been set by Burglinde Pollak from East Germany in 1970. After four events (100-meter hurdles, shot put, high jump, long jump), Britain's Mary Peters was leading Pollak and West Germany's Heide Rosendahl in the close-fought points battle (3,871 to 3,824 and 3,750, respectively). All three women were within striking distance of the world record. The final event was the 200-meter dash: Peters, Pollak, and Rosendahl raced in the same timed heat. Rosendahl finished first. Her time of 22.96 earned her 1,041 points, for a total of 4,791 points and a new world record. However, 1.14 seconds later, Peters crossed the finish line behind Pollack but fast enough to earn 930 points for a total of 4,801, bettering the world mark set by Rosendahl less than two seconds prior. Pollak finished with the bronze medal but would score 4,831 points in a meet the following year, reclaiming the world record she held before the 1972 Games.

In the 1972 Olympic women's pentathlon, Britain's Mary Peters won gold after a close race with East Germany's Burglinde Pollak and West Germany's Heidi Rosendahl.

Down to the Second

In the final event of the decathlon in the 1960 Games in Rome, American Rafer Johnson (above) finished 1.2 seconds behind his rival, Yang Chuan-Kwang from Chinese Taipei (the 12th fastest runner), in the 1,500-meter run, but Johnson still earned enough points to secure the gold medal. While not a new world record, Johnson did break the Olympic mark set by Yang moments earlier.

The pentathlon required the mental and physical toughness of five different athletes combined into the physique of one.

—Jackie Joyner-Kersee (track & field, 1984, 1988, 1992, 1996, 3 gold medals, 1 silver, 2 bronzes)

Q: Some countries now award Olympic medalists with a cash prize. In what Olympic sport was a competitor awarded a cash prize equal to that of winning the event, for not competing in the event?

Hint:

This athlete, the heavy favorite to win, refused to compete. Still, the athlete's country rewarded the athlete for this.

Uh-Oh!

A: Judo

The Iranian judoka Arash Miresmaeili finished fifth at the 2000 Olympic Games in Sydney and was the 2001 and 2003 world champion in the 66-kilogram class. His country even selected him to carry the Iranian flag into the 2004 Olympic Opening Ceremony in Athens.

Iranian judoka Arash Miresmaeili before the 2008 Olympic Games. He was disqualified from the 2004 competition for not making his weight.

When the experienced fighter showed up for the weigh-in 1.8 kilograms (4 lb) heavier than his featherweight class allowed, he was disqualified from the rest of the 2004 competition. Many assumed that he had intentionally disqualified himself rather than face his first-round opponent, Ehud Vaks of Israel, for political or religious reasons. In fact, his post weigh-in comments supported this opinion. Precedent for his actions had been set in 2001 when two other Iranian judokas had refused to fight their Israeli counterparts at the World Judo Championships.

Although Miresmaeili later denied he intentionally disqualified himself, and an International Judo Federation investigation did not hold him culpable, the Iranian sports federation still awarded him $125,000—the same amount awarded the two other 2004 Iranian Olympic champions.

• STAT BOX •

Money for Medals

Prize money offered by nation for Olympic medals, as of 2018 (shown in U.S. dollars):

Country	Gold	Silver	Bronze
Singapore	$1,000,000	$500,000	$250,000
Indonesia	$746,000	$378,000	$188,000
Kazakhstan	$250,000	$150,000	$75,000
Azerbaijan	$248,000	$124,000	$62,000
Italy	$166,000	$83,000	$55,000
Hungary	$125,000	$89,000	$71,000
Russia	$61,000	$38,000	$26,000
France	$55,000	422,000	$14,000
U.S.A.	$37,500	$22,500	$15,000
South Africa	$37,000	$19,000	$7,000
Germany	$22,000	$17,000	$11,000
Canada	$15,000	$11,000	$8,000

Even if Arash defeated his Israeli opponent in five seconds, he still would have become an outcast at home. But no amount of money will ever replace the honor of competition, and judo is all about respect and honor.

—Jimmy Pedro (judo, 1992, 1996, 2000, 2004, 2 bronze medals, 1999 World Champion)

Q: In what track & field event did an athlete break a bone during Olympic competition and still finish with a medal?

Hint:

It was an Olympic silver medal.

A: 4x400-meter relay

In the 2012 Olympic Games during heats of the 4x400-meter relay, U.S. runner Manteo Mitchell (right) hands off the baton to Joshua Mance.

Manteo Mitchell is an American runner who finished fifth in the 400-meter event at the 2012 U.S. track & field Olympic trials. This qualified him to run on the 4x400-meter relay team in the Games' preliminary heats. His time was 44.96 seconds.

At the 2012 Olympic Games in London, Mitchell ran the first leg of the relay and, at approximately 200 meters, he heard a loud snap and felt a pop in his left leg. With grim determination, he finished his portion of the relay, handing off the baton to teammate Joshua Mance. Mitchell's part of the relay was timed at somewhere between 45.7 and a 46.1, slower than he had been capable of, but fast enough to keep the Americans in contention. His teammates completed the race, unaware of Mitchell's injury, and finished with the fastest time ever recorded for an Olympic qualifying heat.

When Mitchell limped off the course, doctors discovered that he had indeed broken his left fibula, the narrow bone on the outside of the lower leg.

For the championship final, Mitchell was replaced by Angelo Taylor (a double gold medalist in the 400-meter hurdles). This foursome ran a great race but lost to the faster runners from the Bahamas. Because Mitchell had been instrumental in the team's result, he also received a silver medal, although he was not on the medal podium for the presentation.

When the U.S. team was invited to visit the White House, President Obama told Mitchell that his story was one of the president's favorite of those Games. Mitchell remains a competitive athlete and is looking toward the 2021 Olympic Games in Tokyo.

• STAT BOX •

Painful Games

Notable Team USA athletes injured at the Olympic Games who continued in the competition:

- **Micki King (diving, 1968, 1972): Broke her arm in 1968 hitting the diving board but finished fourth; won gold in 1972.**
- **Steve Genter (swimming, 1972): Had a collapsed lung but returned to win silver.**
- **Paul Gonzales (boxing, 1984): Broke his wrist in the semifinal but finished with the gold medal.**
- **Greg Louganis (diving, 1976, 1984, 1988): Hit his head on the diving board in 1988 but returned to win gold.**
- **Kerri Strug (gymnastics, 1996): Sprained her ankle but returned to win team gold.**

Q: In Olympic competition, which medal—gold, silver, or bronze—is awarded the most often?

Hint: While medals in the Winter Games are fairly evenly awarded, the medals in the Summer Games are always unevenly distributed.

A: Bronze

Bronze medal fashioned for the 2016 Olympic Summer Games in Rio de Janeiro. Bronze is the most-often awarded Olympic medal.

In most Olympic sports, the top three finishers can be separated from the field using results calculated to the smallest margin or by using tiebreaker procedures that are written into the rule book. Ties are relatively rare and are equally likely to occur in all placings. In single-elimination sports like tennis or badminton, those that lose in the semifinals are often required to compete against each other to determine the bronze medalist, but not always.

In combat sports, such as boxing, judo, wrestling, and taekwondo, the Olympic policy is to use the repechage system—in which the top contenders eliminated in the earlier rounds have a chance to win a bronze but are not required to face off against each other. Not only do both athletes receive bronze medals, but both countries' flags fly during the awards ceremony. This will happen in every weight class in both gender divisions in each of the four combat sports. For this reason, in combat sports, bronze medals are always more numerous than either silver or gold. Their number will likely increase because karate is being added to the 2021 Olympic program. There are no combat sports in the Olympic Winter Games.

• STAT BOX •

Bronze Wins Big

In the Summer Games, more bronze medals are awarded than gold or silver.

Games	Gold	Silver	Bronze
2004 Summer	301	300	326
2006 Winter	84	84	84
2008 Summer	302	303	353
2010 Winter	86	87	85
2012 Summer	301	303	353
2014 Winter	99	95	99
2016 Summer	307	307	359
2018 Winter	103	102	102

Medal-Making

The organizers of the 1896 and 1900 Olympic Games awarded only silver or bronze medals and various cups and trophies to the top finishers. Gold medals were not introduced until 1904 because they were considered too expensive to make. The medals were made of solid gold from 1904 to 1912, and made of silver dipped in gold thereafter.

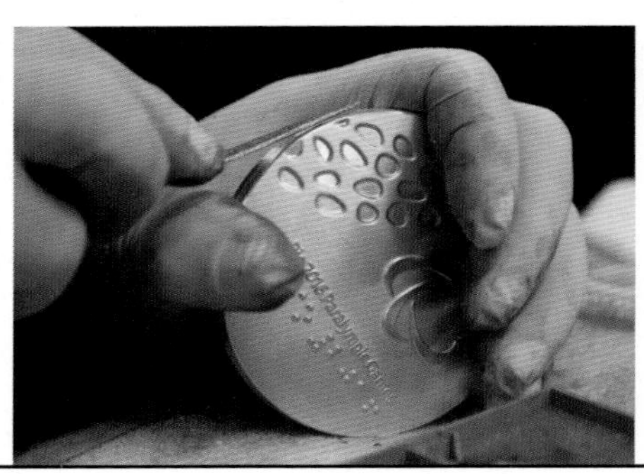

At the Casa da Moeda do Brasil (Brazilian Mint), a medal is sculpted for the 2016 Paralympic events in Rio.

Q: In what sport and event did officials change an athlete's result in order to match another official's interpretation of the event?

Hint: The silver medalist actually went faster than the gold medalist, but the official times were adjusted so the silver medalist's result would not be officially better than that of the gold medalist.

A: Swimming, 100-meter freestyle

This might be the most egregious of all Olympic controversies. The favorite in the men's 100-meter freestyle at the 1960 Olympic Games was Australian John Devitt, the 1956 silver medalist and reigning world record holder. America's hopes rested on the shoulders of Lance Larson who, earlier that year, had become the first man to swim the 100-meter butterfly under 60 seconds.

Australian swimmer John Devitt, (center) receives gold over American Lance Larson (right) after a timing controversy at the 1960 Olympic Games in Rome.

Each lane had three timers with handheld buttons connected to an electronic measuring device. From the side of the pool judges watched the finish line to determine the order of finish: Three judges watched for first place, three judges for second, and so on.

In the final, Larson appeared to reach the wall first. The three timers in his lane clocked him at 55.0, 55.1, and 55.1. All three timers in Devitt's lane clocked the Australian at 55.2 seconds. The six judges in charge of determining the first and second place finishes were evenly split: Three thought Devitt had won, and three saw Larson win.

The chief judge, Henry Runströmer of Sweden, declared Devitt the winner *without having the authority to do so.* As a result, Larson's times were changed (since logically the silver medalist cannot be faster than the gold). Both swimmers were credited with a new Olympic record of 55.2 seconds, but only Devitt was honored with the victory. This dispute precipitated the use of electronic touch pads at all future Olympic Games, and the removal of judges to determine the order of finish.

I have always been taught to accept the judge's decision.

—*Daily Telegraph* quoting John Devitt (swimming, 1956, 1960, 2 gold medals, 1 silver, 1 bronze)

Officials Controversy!

In the 2000 Olympic Games in Sydney, the gymnastics vaulting table was accidentally set five centimeters (2 in) too low during the all-around finals, causing many competitors to fall or land badly and receive lower than usual scores. Among them was Russian Svetlana Khorkina, who had led in the qualifications, then fell on the vault in the finals. Romanian gymnasts evidently adjusted and received the top three medals. At the 2002 Games in Salt Lake City, a French figure skating judge admitted to caving to pressure from her federation to favor a Russian skating pair over a Canadian pair. Once the scandal was revealed, two sets of gold medals were awarded because neither pair of athletes was to blame.

In 2000 Russian gymnast Svetlana Khorkina falls off the improperly set vault.

Q: Which four Americans competed in the 1984 Olympic Games in Los Angeles and then were quickly inducted into the U.S. Olympic Hall of Fame just one year later?

The U.S. Olympic & Paralympic Hall of Fame (as it is now called) currently requires a five-year absence from active competition to be considered for induction, but this rule had not been established in 1985.

A: Track & field stars Edwin Moses and Carl Lewis, diver Greg Louganis, and gymnast Mary Lou Retton

The 1984 Olympic Games were a great success for Team USA primarily because the Games took place on American soil with large, partisan crowds. Also the Soviet Union led a boycott of the Games by many Communist countries, ostensibly due to security concerns though many felt it was in retaliation for the U.S.-led boycott of the 1980 Olympic Games in Moscow. Regardless, the absence of the Soviets and most of the other Communist nations provided a great opportunity for American athletes to shine.

Four-time gold medalist Carl Lewis in 1984

On the track, Carl Lewis won four gold medals, dominating the sprints and long jump. Hurdler Edwin Moses successfully defended the title he earned at the 1976 Games in Montreal. Greg Louganis dominated both the springboard and platform, winning by margins of an entire dive in both events. Mary Lou Retton became a household name thanks to her multiple, perfect-scoring vaults in the all-around competition.

Edwin Moses defends his title in 1984.

The U.S. Olympic & Paralympic Hall of Fame had few restrictive rules when its first class was inducted in 1983. All but Retton later continued their Olympic careers. Louganis competed in 1988, winning two more gold medals. Moses earned a bronze medal in 1988. Lewis's Olympic exploits lasted even longer: He won Olympic gold in 1988, 1992, and 1996.

Mary Lou Retton wins gymnastics individual all-round gold in 1984.

• STAT BOX •

First Hall of Fame Class

The U.S. Olympic & Paralympic Hall of Fame inducted its first class in 1983. Though current classes focus on more recent athletes, at least two "Legends" are inducted each time, along with special "Contributors."

1983

- Al Oerter (discus, 1956, 1960, 1964, 1968)
- Babe Didrikson (track & field, 1932)
- Bob Beamon (long jump, 1968)
- Bob Mathias (decathlon, 1948, 1952)
- Bob Richards (track & field, 1948, 1952, 1956)
- Dick Button (figure skating, 1948, 1952)
- Don Schollander (swimming, 1964, 1968)
- Eddie Eagan (boxing, 1920; bobsled, 1932)
- Eric Heiden (speed skating, 1976, 1980)
- Harrison Dillard (track & field, 1948, 1952)
- Jesse Owens (track & field, 1936)
- Jim Thorpe (track & field, 1912)
- Johnny Weissmuller (swimming and water polo, 1924, 1928)
- Mark Spitz (swimming, 1968, 1972)
- Muhammad Ali (boxing, 1960)
- Peggy Fleming Jenkins (figure skating, 1968)
- Rafer Johnson (track & field, 1956, 1960)
- Ray Ewry (track & field, 1900, 1904, 1908)
- Wilma Rudolph (track & field, 1956, 1960)
- 1980 U.S. ice hockey team
- Avery Brundage (IOC/USOPC)

Q: In what sport did temporary blindness contribute to a competitor earning America's first men's gold medal in that sport in 62 years?

Hint:

The blindness forced the athlete to draw upon other skills.

A: Bobsled

In the most demanding of Olympic speed sports, bobsleds often exceed 145 kilometers an hour (90 mph) and life-changing decisions must be made in fractions of a second. In 2002 American driver Steve Holcomb was diagnosed with keratoconus, a degenerative illness that occasionally causes blindness. In his book, *But Now I See: My Journey From Blindness to Olympic Gold,* Holcomb explains that he was forced to drive by the seat of his pants (by the feel of the sled's runners on the ice). In 2006 he drove the U.S. four-man and two-man sleds in the Torino Olympic Games, finishing 6th and 14th, respectively. Two years later, his illness had progressed so severely (his vision was around 20/1000) that he elected to have operations to stabilize the disease and implant corrective lenses. With his vision restored, his driving, both by sight and feel, improved. On occasion, he'd purposely scuff up his helmet's plastic face mask to reduce clarity and help him return to the instinctive driving of his past. At the 2010 Games in Vancouver, Steve Holcomb and his "Night Train" team of pushers (Steve Mesler, Justin Olsen, and Curtis Tomasevicz) earned the first U.S. gold in Olympic bobsled since 1948. He earned two more silver medals at the 2014 Games in Sochi.

The U.S. four-man bobsled team, riding the "Night Train" driven by Steve Holcomb, takes the gold at the 2010 Olympic Games in Vancouver.

Taylor: A Bobsledding First

It may seem an unusual practice regimen, pushing a 1,590-kilogram (3,500 lb) car with her father sitting in the front seat, but Elana Meyers Taylor's success in Olympic bobsled is also rare. Taylor (above in 2018) is one of only two women in the world to have won three Olympic bobsled medals. She's the only athlete ever to win Olympic medals in both the brakeman and driver positions. And in 2014 she became the first woman to drive a mixed-gender four-person bobsled in international competition.

When you drive by feel, you don't have to think as much.

—Steve Mesler (bobsled, 2002, 2006, 2010, 1 gold medal)

Q: Who was America's first female Olympic figure skating champion?

Hint:

She was also one of Harvard University's early *female* medical students and later became a successful surgeon.

A: Tenley Albright

First female American Olympic figure skating champion, Tenley Albright, at the 1956 Olympic Winter Games in Cortina, Italy

Dick Button was America's first Olympic figure skating champion, winning gold at the 1948 and 1952 Games. Tenley Emma Albright took up figure skating as a way to recover from a polio attack when she was 11. By the time she was 16, she had become one of America's top figure skaters. Albright competed at the 1952 Games in Oslo, Norway, finishing second to Britain's Jeannette Altwegg, and began a four-year run of dominance that included five national titles, two North American titles, two world titles, and two world runner-up finishes.

In 1956, leading up to her second Olympic Winter Games in Cortina, Italy, she fell on the ice in practice and cut her right ankle to the bone; her father, a surgeon, promptly stitched it up. Undaunted, two weeks later, she gave a winning performance at the Winter Games and became the first American woman to win an Olympic figure skating title. She retired from Olympic competition after the 1956 Games, graduated from Harvard Medical School in 1961 (among the school's first female graduates), and became a surgeon shortly thereafter.

• STAT BOX •

Champions on Ice

As of 2020, America's individual figure skating gold medalists are the following:

- Dick Button, 1948, 1952
- Tenley Albright, 1956
- Alan Jenkins, 1956
- Carol Heiss, 1960
- David Jenkins, 1960
- Peggy Fleming, 1968
- Dorothy Hamill, 1976
- Scott Hamilton, 1984
- Brian Boitano, 1988
- Kristi Yamaguchi, 1992
- Tara Lipinski, 1998
- Sarah Hughes, 2002
- Evan Lysacek, 2010

Kerrigan Skates Past Adversity to 1994 Silver Medal

Nancy Kerrigan's road to Olympic success was anything but smooth. Her dad sometimes worked three jobs to fund her skating—one was driving the Zamboni at a local rink to pay for her lessons. She won Olympic bronze at Albertville in 1992, but seven weeks before the 1994 Games she (left, in white) was struck on her right knee with a metal baton wielded by a man hired by rival (in background) Tonya Harding's ex-husband. Kerrigan persevered and won silver at the Olympic Games in Lillehammer.

Q: Besides German gymnast/wrestler Carl Schuhmann in 1896, who is the only Olympian to win gold medals in two different sports at the same Games?

Hint:

Her events took place one week apart during the Olympic Winter Games in 2018.

A: Ester Ledecka

Ester Ledecka is the granddaughter of an Olympic ice hockey player who won medals in 1964 and 1968 playing for Czechoslovakia. For years, she has been a double threat—that is, proficient in two sports—in Alpine skiing and snowboard. In 2014 she just missed qualifying for the Czech Republic Olympic Alpine ski team, but she did compete at the 2014 Winter Games in Sochi in the parallel giant slalom snowboard event. She was eliminated in the quarterfinals by Switzerland's Patrizia Kummer, the eventual Olympic champion that year.

At the 2018 Winter Games in PyeongChang, South Korea, Czech Ester Ledecka runs the snowboard parallel giant slalom course a week after the Alpine super-G. She won gold in both events.

One of the biggest surprises at the 2018 Olympic Winter Games in PyeongChang occurred in the super-G Alpine event. Because of deteriorating snow conditions, the media outlets were declaring Austrian Anna Veith the winner before the entire field had registered their results. Ledecka was seeded 49th, and to the surprise of most onlookers, she roared down the mountain, finishing a hundredth of a second ahead of the leader. Even more amazing was the rumor that the 22-year-old was skiing on borrowed equipment.

One week later, in her other, and perhaps better, sport of snowboard, she dominated both the red and blue courses of the parallel giant slalom, building a 1.26-second lead on the field and qualifying in first place. In the elimination rounds she tore through the competition with no one getting closer to her than 0.46 seconds on her way to her second gold medal. The following day, Ledecka was chosen as her country's flag bearer for the Closing Ceremony.

Winning Attitude

Chris Waddell (below in 2002) has an impressive résumé. After a ski accident left him paralyzed from the waist down, he took Paralympic Alpine skiing by storm. He's won world titles in skiing and track, and his dozen Paralympic Games medals include four golds in 1994. In 2009 he reached the summit of Mount Kilimanjaro in a four-wheel hand cycle. And his attitude is simple but compelling: "It's not what happens to you. It's what you do with what happens to you." Waddell was inducted into the USOP Hall of Fame in 2019.

Q: In what sport did an American-born athlete win two gold medals for Russia in an Olympic Games?

Hint: This athlete would subsequently compete in another Olympic Games under a flag from neither country.

Uh-Oh!

A: Snowboard

Snowboarders Vic Wild, left, and Alena Zavarzina, win three medals for Russia in the 2014 Olympic Winter Games in Sochi, Russia.

Following the 2010 Olympic Games, the U.S. Ski & Snowboard governing body decided to cut the funding allocated to Alpine snowboard events. Vic Wild was just beginning to make a name for himself in the parallel slalom and elected to travel to Russia in order to train with what he felt was the necessary support. In 2011 he married a Russian snowboarder, Alena Zavarzina, herself a world champion, and obtained Russian citizenship in 2012. Wild chose to compete for Russia in the 2014 Olympic Games. Conveniently, the 2014 Olympic Games were scheduled to take place in Sochi, Russia.

With his citizenship obtained, Wild won a bronze medal for Russia at the 2013 World Snowboarding Championships in Canada. The following season, at the 2014 Olympic Games in Sochi, he became the first Olympic snowboarder to win two medals in the same Games when he won both the parallel slalom and parallel giant slalom events. Vladimir Putin awarded Wild the Order for Merit to the Fatherland for his Olympic achievements. Wild's wife, Zavarzina, also earned a bronze medal in the parallel giant slalom at the Sochi Games, competing with a brace on her broken arm from a crash earlier in the season.

Four years later, however, the International Olympic Committee denied Russia the chance to compete at the 2018 Winter Games in PyeongChang because of Russia's tampering with athletes' urine samples used for drug testing in Sochi. Some individual Russian athletes, including Wild and Zavarzina, were allowed to compete under a neutral (Olympic) flag, but neither Wild nor Zavarzina earned a medal at the 2018 Games.

Lost Boy to Flag Bearer

The Sudanese Civil War saw thousands of children from South Sudan orphaned or displaced by genocide. Some 20,000 "Lost Boys" traveled on foot to refugee camps thousands of miles away. Lopepe "Lopez" Lomong spent 10 years in a Kenyan camp before relocating to a family in the United States. He joined his high school track and cross-country teams and helped lead them to sectional and state titles. In 2007 he won NCAA Division I titles in the 1,500- and 3,000-meter events, and on July 6, 2007, he became a U.S. citizen. One year later he was named to the 2008 U.S. Olympic team and was later chosen as the U.S. flag bearer (right) for the Opening Ceremony of the Games in Beijing.

Q: In what sport did a competitor earn a bronze medal while competing with four broken ribs and a collapsed lung?

Hint: The injury occurred minutes before the start of the event.

A: Cross-country skiing

Petra Majdič was a cross-country skier for Slovenia at the 2002, 2006, and 2010 Olympic Winter Games. On the morning of February 17, 2010, as she was preparing for the heats of the 1.4-kilometer classic sprint race, she accidentally skied off course and tumbled down a three-meter (10 ft) ditch, breaking her skis and poles and unknowingly cracking four ribs. A cursory physical examination found no reason that she should not compete, so, after a short delay, she fought her way through the qualifying heats before collapsing and being sent to the hospital. The ultrasound failed to spot any broken bones, so she returned to the competition that afternoon and won her quarterfinal. In the semifinals, an undiagnosed broken rib punctured her lung, collapsing it, and she finished among the slowest to advance to the final. In spite of the pain, Majdič insisted on competing in the final where, in her fourth race in four hours, she was able to summon the strength and courage to finish third, thereby becoming Slovenia's first ever Winter Olympic medalist. She attended her medal ceremony with a tube in her chest to relieve the collapsed lung.

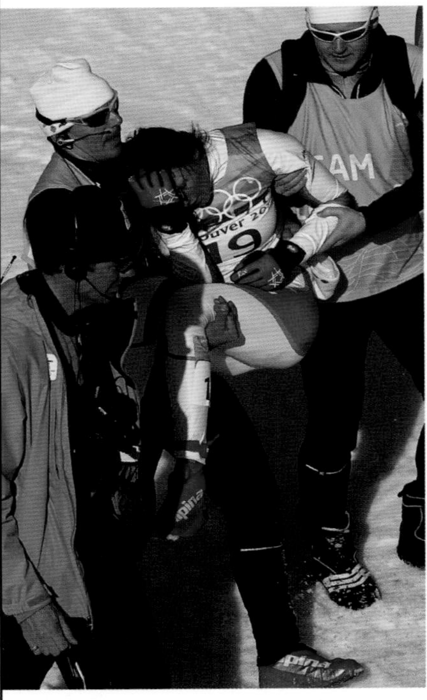

After competing with injuries and winning bronze in cross-country skiing, Slovenia's first ever female medalist, Petra Majdič, is carried off the 2010 Vancouver course.

Today, this is not a bronze. This is a gold with little diamonds on it.

—Petra Majdič, upon receiving the Olympic bronze medal

Kneecap Secret

In the 1976 men's gymnastics team competition, Japan's Shun Fujimoto performed on the pommel horse and still rings while keeping the secret of a broken kneecap incurred during the floor exercise in the first rotation. His dismount from the rings was an eight-foot drop from a triple somersault, and he "stuck" his landing long enough to earn 9.7 from the judges, helping his team win the gold medal over the Soviet Union by 0.4 points.

Despite a broken kneecap, Japanese gymnast Shun Fujimoto delivers a gold-medal-worthy performance at the 1976 Olympic Games in Montreal.

Q: In what Olympic sport did an athlete move from fifth (last) place to first in the final 1.5 seconds of the competition?

Hint:

The winner had overcome much worse odds in his past and later published a book titled *Last Man Standing*.

A: Short track speed skating

Short track involves jockeying for position around very tight turns, and crashes are frequent.

Steven Bradbury was a skater on four Australian Olympic teams. In 1994 in Lillehammer, Norway, he helped Australia earn its first Olympic Winter Games medal. In an event in Montreal, another skater's blade cut through all four quadriceps muscles of Bradbury's right thigh, and he lost four liters of blood. In 2000 he was in a training accident that fractured his C4 and C5 vertebrae. Doctors were sure he'd never skate competitively again. But in 2002 Bradbury qualified for his fourth Olympic team, at the age of 30—the second-oldest competitor in the field.

At the 2002 Olympic Winter Games, Australian speed skater Steven Bradbury wins gold, with America's Apolo Ohno claiming silver.

Bradbury's strategy was to be fast enough to advance but not to get involved in any on-ice accidents. He rightly assumed that the final would be a tight fight for the gold medal. When the group approached the final turn, Bradbury was 15 meters behind the leaders. Then, one of the lead skaters slipped on the ice and slid across the path of the others, knocking them all off their feet. Bradbury avoided the pile-up and crossed the finish line standing upright with his arms raised. He earned the Southern Hemisphere's first Olympic Winter Games gold medal. American Apolo Ohno—one of the downed skaters—took the silver because he was faster at getting up than the other skaters. Bradbury was hailed for his "never give up" spirit and his book, *Last Man Standing,* was released to an appreciative audience.

• STAT BOX •

Coming From Behind

Some notable "come-from-behind" U.S. Olympic finishes:

- **1964, Tokyo, track & field:** Bob Hayes in the 4x100-meter relay runs the fastest relay split ever (8.6 seconds) to pass three teams and win his second gold medal, and Billy Mills in the 10,000 meters goes from eighth to first in the final 10 seconds.
- **1972, Munich, track & field:** Dave Wottle in the 800-meter run goes from fourth to first in the final six seconds.
- **2008, Beijing, swimming:** Anchor Jason Lezak in the 4x100-meter freestyle relay comes from a half second behind to win by eight-hundredths of a second to help Michael Phelps win his second of eight gold medals.
- **2016, Rio de Janeiro, swimming:** Maya DiRado overcomes a half-second deficit in the final 50 meters of the 200-meter backstroke to win gold by six-hundredths of a second.

Short track is like life. We can plan and prepare, but results are not within our control. How we respond and reengage, is.

—Apolo Ohno (short track speed skating, 2002, 2006, 2010, 2 gold medals, 2 silvers, 4 bronzes)

Q: In what event did four different Paralympic competitors outperform the Olympic gold medalist's result the same year?

Hint:

The Olympic champion made a strategic decision in order to win the gold medal.

A: 1,500-meter run

At the 2016 Olympic Games in Rio de Janeiro, U.S. runner Matt Centrowicz (son of the 1976 Olympic runner by the same name) ran both his preliminary heat and semifinal faster than 3:40. He was known for his "finishing kick" and for the final, he decided to run a more strategic race, slowing the field early in the race, conserving energy for a sprint at the finish. His decision proved wise as he outraced the field down the home stretch and was declared the winner. He'd run the race in 3:50.00, the slowest Olympic winning time since 1932, and beating the next three finishers by less than three-tenths of a second.

Algerian runner Abdellatif Baka celebrates his gold medal for the 1,500-meter run at the 2016 Paralympic Games in Rio de Janeiro.

A few weeks later, at the Paralympic Games on the same course, in the T-13 (visually impaired) classification, four different runners covered the same distance in faster times than Centrowicz. The winner, Abdellatif Baka of Algeria, clocked in at 3:48.29—1.7 seconds faster than the able-bodied Olympic gold medalist's time.

Fourth place in the same event went to Baka's brother, Fouad Baka, whose time of 3:49.84, was also faster than the Olympic champion's winning time.

We develop strategies to compensate for our vision impairment through our preparation.

—Marla Runyan
(Paralympic track & field 1992, 1996, Olympic track & field, 2000, 2004)

Wheelchair Tennis Champion

Brad Parks's dream of being a pro skier ended at age 18 when an icy spill left him paralyzed from the hips down. In the hospital he began thinking about how to stay active, which led him to essentially invent the sport of wheelchair tennis. He was ranked number one in the world from 1980 to 1989, helped get the sport into the Paralympic Games, and then won gold in doubles in 1992 with 2004 USOP Hall of Fame inductee Randy Snow.

International Tennis Hall of Famer and Paralympic doubles champion Brad Parks in 2014

Q: Which U.S. Paralympic athlete was also America's top performer at an event in the Olympic Games?

Hint:

This multiple Paralympic medalist competed in different events at the Paralympic and Olympic Games.

WOW!

A: Marla Runyan

At the 2000 Olympic Games in Sydney, U.S. runner Marla Runyan, far right, was the fastest American woman in the 1,500-meter event.

Marla Runyan is legally blind, and after winning four gold medals in sprints and long jump at the 1992 Paralympic Games in Barcelona, she tried her luck competing against able-bodied athletes. Runyan attempted to make the U.S. Olympic team in the heptathlon at the 1996 U.S. Olympic Team trials, a sport with seven events (100-meter hurdles, high jump, shot put, 200-meter run, long jump, javelin throw, and 800-meter run). Her remarkable result in the 800-meter run (she set a new American record for all athletes in the heptathlon) taught her that she had even greater potential as a distance runner. She won gold in the 1,500 meters at the 1999 Pan American Games in Canada and went on to earn a spot on the 2000 and 2004 U.S. Olympic track teams in the same 1,500-meter run. At the 2000 Sydney Games she was the fastest American woman in that event. In 2001 she won her first of three national titles in the 5,000-meter run. In 2019 Runyan was nominated for induction into the U.S. Olympic & Paralympic Hall of Fame, and though she was not elected, she may well be inducted at a future date.

Heroes

Military veterans Dan Cnossen and Andy Soule both lost their legs to improvised explosive devices in Afghanistan. Years later they stood together on a podium at the 2018 PyeongChang Paralympic Games, both having won medals in the 12.5-kilometer (sitting) biathlon event. Earlier, in the biathlon pursuit in 2010, Soule had become the first American to win a biathlon medal at the Olympic or Paralympic Games. Cnossen would win six medals at the 2018 Paralympic Games, and would became the first American man to win biathlon gold (in the 7.5-kilometer event).

U.S. biathlete Dan Cnossen at the 2018 Paralympic Winter Games in PyeongChang, South Korea

Andy Soule was the trailblazer.... When I was new on the team, he was the inspiration."

—Dan Cnossen (biathlon, cross-country skiing, 2014, 2018, 1 gold medal, 4 silvers, 1 bronze)

Q: The 1984 Olympic Games in Los Angeles introduced Paralympic competition to the fans during what established Olympic sport?

Hint:

The two exhibition events took place on the existing facilities.

A: Track & field

Until 1992, host countries were allowed to add demonstration sports to the Olympic schedule as a way of introducing their national sports to the world. For instance, the 1984 Games in Los Angeles reintroduced U.S.-favored baseball and tennis as demonstration sports (hoping eventually to see them added to the Olympic program). They also added exhibition events in the existing Olympic sport of track & field: the men's 1,500-meter and women's 800-meter wheelchair races. American wheelchair athletes Randy Snow (wheelchair racing, 1984; tennis, 1992; basketball, 1996; tennis, 2000, for three Paralympic medals) and Candace Cable (wheelchair racing, 1980, 1984, 1988, 1992, 1996; Alpine skiing, 1992; and cross-country skiing: 1994, 1998, 2002, 2006, for 12 Paralympic medals) both earned exhibition medals, and each has since been inducted into the U.S. Olympic & Paralympic Hall of Fame.

Sweden's Monica Saker wins silver in the women's 800-meter wheelchair race at the 1984 Summer Games in Los Angeles.

Chinese Taipei Kuo Tai-yuan pitches against the United States at the 1984 Olympic Games.

Demonstration vs. Exhibition Competitions

Demonstration sports are not currently on the Olympic program but have been added by the host country to demonstrate a favorite national sport, such as American baseball or Korean taekwondo. Exhibition events are contests that occur in featured Olympic sports but are not included in that year's program. Medals awarded in either demonstration sports or exhibition events do not appear in the official Olympic results.

I was a part of a shift in perspective, on so many levels for so many people.

—Candace Cable, Olympic track, 1984, 1988, 1992, 2 bronze medals; Paralympic track, 1980, 1988, 1992, 1996; Alpine skiing, 1992; Nordic skiing, 1994, 1998, 2002, 2006, 8 gold medals, 2 silvers, 2 bronzes)

Q: The first person to win a medal in both Olympic and Paralympic competition did so in which sport(s)?

Hint: He did it using very similar equipment, beginning in 1988.

A: Fencing and wheelchair fencing

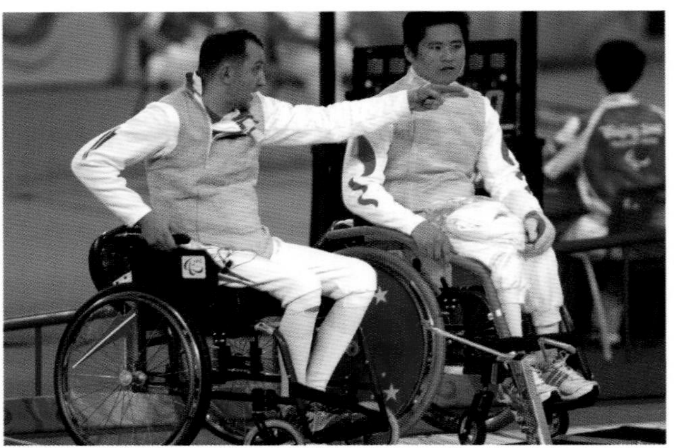

Hungary's Pál Szekeres, left, with eventual champion, China's Hu Daoliang, before fencing in Beijing, 2008

Pál Szekeres earned a bronze medal in Olympic fencing as part of the 1988 Hungarian team foil event. He was injured in a bus accident three years later and confined to a wheelchair. He returned to competitive shape while still confined to the chair, in time to earn gold at the 1992 Paralympic Games in Barcelona and two more golds at the 1996 Paralympic Games in Atlanta. He also medaled in 2000, 2004, and 2008. He is sometimes described as "the most successful Paralympic athlete in Hungary."

• STAT BOX •

Italian Fencers and the World Wars

- **Before WWI:** Italian fencer Nedo Nadi won the individual foil gold medal at the 1912 Games in Stockholm.
- **During WWI:** The 1916 Games were canceled.
- **After WWI:** Nedo returned to win five gold medals—the only fencer to win gold with all three weapons in a single Games.
- **Before WWII:** Edoardo Mangiarotti won an épée team gold for Italy in 1936.
- **During WWII:** Mangiarotti had to wait eight years before he returned to the Olympic fencing strip.
- **After WWII:** From 1948 to 1960, Mangiarotti earned an additional five gold, five silver, and two bronze medals. The IOC deemed him the greatest fencer of all time.

My system of defense was not nearly as clock-like as that of Nedo. However, more varied and simpler, it proved to be, in time, at least as efficient as his and certainly more baffling. Its very flexibility was its most valuable asset.

—Aldo Nadi, brother of Nedo (fencing, 1920, 3 gold medals, 1 silver)

Paralympic Fencing

Paralympians use the same weapons that are used in the Olympic Games: épée, foil, and sabre. Their movements fall into two classifications: full trunk movement with good balance versus limited trunk movement and impaired balance. Women do not compete in the saber event. Both genders compete in team events as well as individual events. The wheelchairs are anchored to the ground for Paralympic competitions.

Paralympic fencers China's Jing Bian, left, and Poland's Marta Fidrych, in women's individual épée match at the Rio Games in 2016

Q: In what sport did a Paralympian first compete in the Olympic Games against able-bodied athletes?

Hint:

The parts of the athlete's body that were not in full working order were less critical in this sport.

A: Archery

New Zealand archer Neroli Fairhall competed in the 1984 Olympic Games in Los Angeles.

New Zealander Neroli Fairhall was a competitive athlete before being injured in a motorcycle accident that left her paralyzed below the waist. At the 1972 Paralympic Games, she competed in track & field events, and in 1980 in both track and archery, winning a gold medal with her bow and arrows. At the 1982 Commonwealth Games she earned another gold medal in archery against able-bodied athletes. The following year she was appointed a member of the Order of the British Empire by Queen Elizabeth II. In 1984 she represented her country at the Olympic Games in Los Angeles and finished 35th out of 47 competitors. She would also compete in archery at the 1988 and 2000 Paralympic Games before becoming a coach at her archery club in Christchurch, New Zealand. She passed away in 2006.

Archers often take their legs for granted, but they are the foundation for your control.

—Justin Huish (archery, 1996, 2 gold medals)

Abebe Bikila

Ethiopia's Abebe Bikila (below) became the first Sub-Saharan African Olympic champion when he won the 1960 Olympic marathon in Rome, running barefoot. Four years later, he successfully defended his Olympic title, but in 1969 he was injured in a car accident that left him in a wheelchair for the rest of his life. In 1970 he competed in a precursor to the Paralympic Games, in archery and table tennis. He was denied the chance to compete at the 1972 Paralympic Games in Heidelberg, Germany, when his Ethiopian teammates failed to arrive in time.

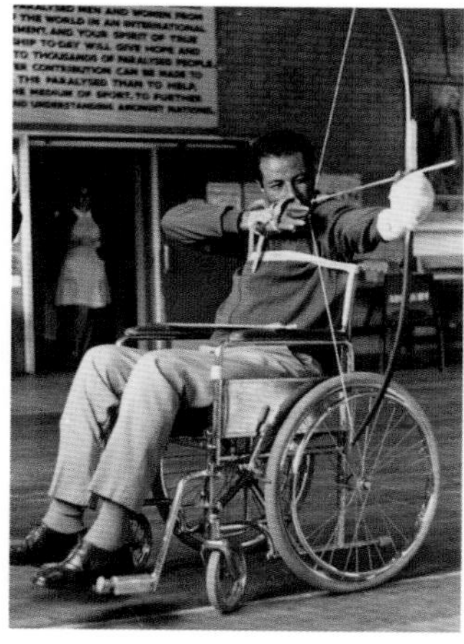

Q: Who is the only Paralympian to have the honor of being the last person to receive the Olympic flame and of lighting the cauldron at an Olympic Opening Ceremony?

Hint:

He did not carry the flame very far, nor did he ever get close to the Olympic cauldron.

A: Antonio Rebollo

Born in Madrid, Spain, Antonio Rebollo was afflicted with polio just months before his first birthday and lost the full use of both his legs. In spite of this handicap, he loved challenges. Because running and kicking sports were out of the question, he took up archery. Rebollo competed at the Paralympic Games in 1984 and again in 1988, winning a silver and a bronze medal, respectively. Organizers for the 1992 Games in Barcelona were looking for an archer to launch a flaming arrow to light the cauldron during the Opening Ceremony, and Rebollo was among 200 candidates for the job. For days he prepared, shooting hundreds of arrows in a variety of weather conditions, flames occasionally singeing his fingers. His success rate in practice was a little better than 50 percent. Two hours before the fateful moment, the decision came down: Rebollo received the honor.

The Olympic flame came into the stadium and eventually made its way onto the torch of Spanish basketball superstar Juan Antonio

Spanish archer Antonio Rebollo aims his flaming arrow at the cauldron for the opening of the 1992 Olympic Games.

The time-lapse trail of Rebollo's flaming arrow lighting the Olympic cauldron in Barcelona

"Epi" San Epifanio, who jogged to the elevated stage where Rebollo was waiting. The flame was passed from Epi's torch to the fuel-dipped gauze that encased the tip of Antonio's arrow. Rebollo pulled back his bow's string, and it seemed that people around the globe held their breath for this climactic event. The arrow leapt off the bow and soared over the heads of rows of spectators, gracefully gliding across the top of the cauldron, igniting the flame that glowed for the duration of those Games.

At the Paralympic Games later that year, Rebollo added to his medal count with a silver-medal performance in the men's team open event.

I was nervous just handing off the flame to Muhammad Ali. If I had to shoot an arrow over the heads of hundreds of spectators, I think I might have fainted.

—Janet Evans (swimming, 1988, 1992, 1996, 4 gold medals, 1 silver, second-to-last torchbearer in 1996)

INTERNATIONAL OLYMPIC COMMITTEE

Q: Since 1920, during the Olympic Opening Ceremony a representative of the host country's team is required to hold a corner of the Olympic flag and speak the Olympic Oath, promising to abide by the rules on behalf of all the competitors. Since 2012, two other representatives have also been included. What groups do they represent?

Neither group is scheduled to compete in the Games, although they do participate.

A: Coaches and officials

The ancient Olympic Games were created as a way to honor the gods on Mount Olympus. The founder of the modern Olympic Games, Pierre de Coubertin, was otherwise inclined. His vision: to use the Games for the improvement of society. He called on the participants to compete honorably in the spirit of sportsmanship and fair play. In 1972 the Games required the volunteer officials and referees to likewise abide by the high Olympian standards. By 2012, with the introduction of the Youth Olympic Games, the coaches were included as well, because these are the people the athletes most regard. Currently all three groups, each represented by an individual, proclaim the oath simultaneously during the Opening Ceremony while touching the Olympic flag.

At the Rio Opening Ceremony in 2016, Brazilians Robert Scheidt, Adriana Santos, and Martinho Nobre, not pictured, take the Olympic Oath on behalf of athletes, coaches, and referees.

The Olympic Oath

Although it has changed through time, as of 2018 the oath is:

We promise to take part in these Olympic Games, respecting and abiding by the rules and in the spirit of fair play. We all commit ourselves to sport without doping and cheating. We do this for the glory of sport, for the honor of our teams, and in respect for the Fundamental Principles of Olympism.

George Calnan, U.S. fencing team captain, takes the Olympic Oath, Los Angeles, 1932.

• STAT BOX •

Oath Takers

In 2002 bobsledder Jimmy Shea took the Olympic Oath for all the athletes in Salt Lake City. His grandfather, speed skater Jack Shea, had done so 70 years prior in Lake Placid. Both earned gold medals. These Americans have also taken the oath:

- 1932 Los Angeles: George Calnan (fencing, 1920, 1924, 1928, 1932, 3 bronze medals)
- 1960 Squaw Valley: Carol Heiss (figure skating, 1956, 1960, 1 gold, 1 silver)
- 1980 Lake Placid: Eric Heiden (speed skating, 1980, 5 golds)
- 1984 Los Angeles: Edwin Moses (track & field, 1976, 1984, 1988, 2 golds, 1 bronze)
- 1996 Atlanta: Teresa Edwards (basketball, 1984, 1988, 1992, 1996, 2000, 4 golds, 1 bronze)

Q: In what Olympic team sport did the judges award all 10s to the entire team?

Hint:

The winning team enjoyed a home court advantage.

A: Synchronized swimming

In 1996 the U.S. women's synchronized swimming team won Olympic gold at the Atlanta Centennial Games, with a perfect score for their free routine.

The 1996 Centennial Olympic Games in Atlanta saw the solo and duet events in synchronized swimming replaced by the single team event for the first time. The United States was favored because of their victory in the prior world championships as well as the obvious home court advantage. The free routine counted for 65 percent of the overall score, while the technical routine counted for 35 percent. On July 30, eight U.S. women (Tammy Cleland, Becky Dyroen-Lancer, Heather Pease, Jill Savery, Nathalie Schneyder, Jill Sudduth, Emily LeSueur, and Margot Thien) delivered a spectacular technical performance, receiving many 9s and a few 10s on a 0–10.0 scale. Three days later, in the free routine, the group of eight (with Suzannah Bianco and Heather Simmons-Carrasco replacing LeSueur and Thien) competed before a panel of 10 judges. Nine judges awarded the U.S. team a 10.0, giving them 65 of the 65 possible points (after dropping the high and low scores). This performance earned America the first synchro team gold medal ever awarded at the Games. The duet event joined the team event on the Olympic program in 2000, and every Games since.

Free vs. Technical

In synchronized (now known as "artistic") swimming, technical routines must include five predetermined elements, including a head-first throw and cadence action, and are judged on the basis of execution, impression, and the mastery of required elements. Team technical routines are limited to 2 minutes 40 seconds in length. The free routines have no requirement on elements or restrictions on choreography, and may last up to four minutes. These routines usually demonstrate creativity and innovation. They are judged on the basis of execution, artistic impression, and difficulty.

The Greek synchronized swimming team performs in the finals at the 2004 Olympic Games in Athens.

Q: What was the first official Olympic mascot?

Hint: It was a breed of animal associated with the host country.

A: Waldi the dachshund, for the 1972 Olympic Games, Munich

Marketing and licensing rights were just becoming valuable in the 1960s and '70s, and the 1968 Olympic Winter Games in Grenoble used an unofficial mascot named Schuss, a male figure on skis with a red head. Waldi the dachshund became the first official mascot, designed for the 1972 Olympic Games in Munich by Otto "Otl" Aicher, a popular graphic designer who had also had a hand in designing the Lufthansa Airlines logo. Waldi was based on a model—a long-haired dachshund named Cherie von Birkenhof—and was supposed to embody the attributes of resistance, tenacity, and agility. Originally, Waldi's colors were to match those of the Olympic rings, but Aicher elected to drop red and black because those colors were associated with the old Nazi party. The first Paralympic mascots were two squirrels, Noggi and Joggi, the symbols for the 1980 World Disabled Games in Arnhem, Netherlands. Mascots (usually in the form of plush dolls and plastic toys) are a way of engaging the youth of the world with the Olympic Games, and the licensing rights generate significant funds for the organizing committees.

A dachsund model posed for the artists making souvenirs of Waldi, the official mascot for the Munich Games of 1972.

• STAT BOX •

Memorable Mascots

Olympic and Paralympic Games mascots have included plants, animals, and imaginary characters.

- 1976, Montreal, Canada, Amik the beaver, Olympic Games
- 1980, Moscow, Russia, Misha the bear, Olympic Games
- 1984, Los Angeles, U.S.A., Sam the eagle, Olympic Games
- 1996, Atlanta, U.S.A., Izzy (short for "What is he?"), Olympic Games
- 2000, Sydney, Australia, Olly the kookaburra, Syd the platypus, and Millie the echidna, Olympic Games
- 2002, Salt Lake City, U.S.A., Powder the snowshoe hare, Copper the coyote, and Coal the black bear, Olympic Games; and Otto the otter, Paralympic Games
- 2004, Athens, Greece, Proteas the sea god, Paralympic Games
- 2016, Rio de Janeiro, Brazil, Vinicius (a cat/monkey/bird hybrid), Olympic Games; and Tom (a version of Brazilian plant life), Paralympic Games
- 2021 Tokyo, Japan, Maraitowa (a teleporting futuristic character), Olympic Games; and Someity (a flying telepath), Paralympic Games

Waldi Marathon Route

The Munich Olympic organizers decided to design the marathon route in the image of a silhouette of the mascot Waldi (below), facing west. Runners began at the dog's neck, and ran the route counterclockwise, ending with a long straightaway into the Olympic stadium.

Q: In what Opening Ceremony was the Olympic flag accidentally raised upside down?

Hint:

The mistake was not seen as a political protest.

A: 1984 Olympic Winter Games, Sarajevo

In 1978 Sarajevo, Yugoslavia, won out against Sapporo, Japan, and Gothenburg, Sweden, for the right to host the 1984 Olympic Winter Games.

By most accounts, the Sarajevo Games were well organized, but there was an unintentional blunder during the final hour of the Opening Ceremony. After the Parade of Nations and just before the entrance of the Olympic flame, the Olympic flag was being attached to the flagpole. During this moment of high drama in Koševo City Stadium, the wrong corner of the flag was clipped onto the first ring of the rope. The crowd of 50,000 watched in dismay as the Olympic flag began to fly with the five-ring symbol appearing upside down.

The stadium was almost destroyed during the Bosnian War that raged in Sarajevo between 1992 and 1995. It is currently being used as the home stadium for the FK (Fudbalski Klub) Sarajevo professional soccer team.

The Olympic flag runs up the flagpole upside down during the Opening Ceremony of the 1984 Olympic Winter Games in Sarajevo, Yugoslavia.

Flag Mix-up

Just days before the start of the 2012 Olympic Games in London, a preliminary women's soccer match between Colombia and North Korea took place in a stadium near Glasgow, Scotland. As the North Korean women entered the field, their images were posted on a large digital scoreboard with the South Korean flag (left) posted alongside them by mistake. The entire team left the arena, refusing to play, until a very contrite organizing committee promised to rectify the situation. British prime minister David Cameron said it was "an honest mistake." The game resumed after a one-hour delay, and the North Koreans won the match 2–0. North Korea finished ninth in the Olympic tournament; the United States took gold.

Q: After the 1972 Israeli Olympic team massacre in Munich, the International Olympic Committee (IOC) was urged to cancel the remaining events. What was the compromise?

Hint: Every event did take place, eventually.

A: The IOC decided to postpone the remaining events by 24 hours.

On September 5, 1972, a group of Palestinian terrorists climbed over a fence separating the Olympic Village from the public, storming into the compound and taking 11 members of the Israeli Olympic team hostage. An unsuccessful rescue attempt resulted in the death of all the Israeli hostages and most of the terrorists. Some of the public called for the remaining Olympic events to be canceled out of respect for the dead.

In 1972 the president of the IOC was Avery Brundage, a 1912 track & field Olympian and former president of the U.S. Olympic Committee (USOC) from 1927 to 1953. During his term at the helm of the U.S. team, Brundage was a stalwart supporter of "the Olympic movement at all costs."

When the Israeli massacre took place, it was the unyielding resolve of Brundage that allowed the Games to continue. In his remarks at the memorial service for the Israeli athletes and guards, he articulated the mood of the crowd when he said "the Games must go on." After the service, he authorized a 24-hour delay in all events, and the Games resumed the following day. This compromise seemed to mollify those who wanted to cancel the Games altogether.

Police in a standoff with Palestine's Black September terrorist group after the Israeli team was taken hostage at the Olympic Village in Munich, 1972.

Avery Brundage

To ensure that the Games and his vision of sportsmanship prevailed, Avery Brundage (above) advocated against boycotting Hitler and the 1936 Games in Berlin and against allowing athletes to earn money for their athletic accomplishments. The latter earned him the nickname "Slavery Brundage." When he became president of the IOC in 1952, he opposed returning the medals won by Jim Thorpe in 1912, confiscated because of Thorpe's earlier participation in a semi-professional baseball league. He also opposed canceling the 1968 Olympic Games after some rioting students were shot and killed. That same year, he insisted that John Carlos and Tommie Smith be expelled from the Olympic Village and the U.S. team after their protest on the medal podium in support of the civil rights movement.

They're all gone.

—ABC Sports announcer Jim McKay, on the loss of the Israeli hostages

Q: In 1976 a gold medalist pulled the silver medalist onto the top step as the national anthem played. The reason for this also helped create new Olympic events. What was the reason?

Hint: The two athletes were from the same country but very different in other ways.

A: In a sport dominated by men, a woman earned the silver medal, which led to the creation of shooting events specifically for women.

At the 1976 Olympic Games, all shooting events were "mixed," meaning that women competed equally with the men, although no woman had ever won an Olympic shooting medal. That year, the 50-meter rifle 3 positions event featured two Americans vying for the gold medal. When the final scores were tabulated, Lanny Bassham and Margaret Murdock had the same score (1,162 out of a possible 1,200), but because of the tiebreaker rules in effect (see sidebar), Bassham was deemed the champion. Murdock became the first woman in history to win a shooting medal in Olympic competition. Bassham asked that two gold medals be awarded, but the officials refused. As "The Star Spangled Banner" began to play, Bassham invited Murdock to join him on the top step of the medal podium, and both athletes stood side by side to enjoy their patriotic moment. Shortly thereafter, the governing body of the sport elected to split the women from the men in most of the shooting events, and by 1984 the Olympic Games featured three new events (10-meter air rifle, 25-meter air pistol, and 50-meter rifle 3 positions) limited only to the female competitors. At the 2016 Games in Rio de Janeiro, the sport featured nine events for the men and six for the women.

U.S. shooting champions Margaret Murdock and Lanny Bassham share the top step of the medal podium at the 1976 Games in Montreal. Germany's Werner Seibold won bronze.

Tiebreaker Rules

At the Montreal Games in 1976, the tiebreaker rules for shooting events were clear even though many of the athletes thought them unfair. In the case of equal scores, the tie for the gold medal (above) would be broken by the shooter with the highest score over the last 10 shots. In 1974 this same rule had cost Bassham a gold medal at the world championships. The tie-breaker rules were changed following the 1976 Games. In addition, the formerly mixed shooting competitions were separated into men's and women's events.

I could practice with the K(ansas)-State team but I couldn't be on the team. They got a new coach and he thought it would be a good idea for me to be on the team since I was shooting better than everyone else.

—Margaret Murdock
(shooting, 1976, 1 silver medal)

Q: In which sport was an Olympic medal refused?

Hint:

It was a team event, and every member of that team agreed to boycott the medal ceremony.

A: Basketball, in 1972

At the 1972 Olympic Games in Munich, the championship game in basketball matched the Soviet Union against the United States. At the time, sporting competitions between the two superpowers were filled with animosity and political symbolism. The world watched with amazement as the two teams were one point apart with seconds remaining. The Soviets led the Americans throughout the game, but with three seconds on the clock, Doug Collins sank two free throws to take the lead for the first time. The Soviets promptly inbounded the ball while their coach signaled for a time out, and a buzzer sounded, implying the end of the game. In a surprise decision, the general secretary of the Basketball Federation, William Jones from Great Britain, stepped out of the crowd and ordered the scorekeepers to put three seconds back on the clock, giving the Soviets a second chance. The second inbound pass was then launched toward the basket but bounced off the backboard just as the buzzer sounded a second time. Amazingly, it was determined that the referee put the ball in play before the clock had been officially reset, so the play would not count. Once again, three seconds were put back on the clock, and this time the long pass found Aleksandr Belov, who shook off his defenders and put the ball in the hoop, ending the game with the Soviets winning 51–50. Believing the unprecedented added time was unfair play and a violation of the rules, the U.S. team members refused their silver medals and boycotted the medal ceremony.

The 1972 Olympic Games medal podium for men's basketball remains partially vacant when the U.S. team refuses the silver medal after a series of controversial decisions awarded gold to the Soviet team.

Silver in Storage

The U.S.-U.S.S.R. competition was the first American defeat in Olympic basketball in 63 games over 36 years. No U.S. team member came out for the medal ceremony, and the silver medals were not presented. The medals (left) remain at the International Olympic Committee headquarters in Lausanne, available for any member of the U.S. team who wants to claim them.

Q: Throughout Olympic history, only one final torchbearer also went on to win a gold medal in the same Games. Who was it?

Hint:

On this occasion, during the athlete's best event, almost everyone in the stadium was rooting for this person. When the athlete won, the roar of the crowd was deafening.

A: Cathy Freeman

Australia's Cathy Freeman crosses the finish line to win gold in the 400-meter final at the 2000 Games in Sydney.

Olympic Games organizers usually choose the final runner in the Olympic Torch Relay from among a short list of the host nation's favorite athletes. Freeman was a national favorite for various reasons: She was the first indigenous Australian to win a gold medal at the Commonwealth Games, in 1990. She was both the silver medalist at the 1996 Olympic Games and the 1999 World Champion in the 400-meter run. Her reputation was as a humble, talented, and hard-working athlete who loved her country and her people, and they loved her in return.

The Sydney Olympic stadium was built to hold 110,000 spectators, making it the largest stadium in Olympic history. The lighting of the Olympic cauldron was a spectacular production, with Freeman appearing to stand on water with her torch before lighting an enormous ring of flames that slowly rose to the top of the stadium. Every Australian had a reason to be proud of that magnificent moment.

On September 25, 2000, day 11 of those Games, a record 112,524 people jammed into the stadium to watch the Australian favorite in her best event. Almost everyone in the stadium was rooting for the Australian and, when Freeman pulled away from the field in the final meters, winning the race by 0.47 seconds, the crowd roar may have been the loudest ever heard at any sporting event.

All Are Winners

In most large public sporting events, half of the audience usually leaves the venue feeling a little disappointed because one team has to lose. The Olympic Games are usually much more rewarding, however, because most of the spectators don't care very much who wins, unless their country has a legitimate candidate for the title. For every 50 countries represented in the crowd, only 10 percent have a horse in the race. In the case of Cathy Freeman (right), because of her personality, character, and role in the Opening Ceremony, almost everyone in the arena was delighted to see her win. Can you imagine the sound of 112,000 people joyfully yelling at the top of their lungs?

Q: Which single Olympic Games took place on two different continents?

Hint:

Regulations in the host country required one of the sports to be relocated.

A: 1956 Olympic Games

The 1956 Games were awarded to Melbourne, Australia, but laws to protect the country's unique natural habitats and unique animal populations required a mandatory six-month quarantine of any animal that might be shipped to the continent. Consequently, the equestrian events had to be relocated to a less restrictive country. Stockholm, the capital of Sweden, had hosted the Games in 1912 and agreed to host the equestrian events a few months after the rest of the Olympic Games took place in Australia.

Equestrian events for the 1956 Olympic Games took place in Stockholm, Sweden (right and below), because of Australia's strict quarantine laws governing animals.

Rio Equestrian Events

In Rio de Janeiro's 2016 Olympic Games, 200 competitors from 43 nations competed in the equestrian events. The 18 medals awarded were shared among seven nations. Four equestrians earned multiple medals in Rio: the United Kingdom's Charlotte Dujardin (above) and Germany's Isabell Werth, Kristina Bröring-Sprehe, and Michael Jung. When Dujardin added a team dressage silver and individual gold in Rio to her two gold medals from London, she became Britain's most decorated Olympic rider in history.

Can we get married now?

—Message worn by Charlotte Dujardin's fiancée, Dean Golding, after she won her Rio gold medal

Q: In what sport did multiple teams intentionally try to lose their Olympic match?

Hint:

They were trying to lose the game in order to win an Olympic medal in the tournament.

Uh-Oh!

A: Badminton, in 2012

At the 2012 Olympic Games in London, spectators who paid good money for their tickets were amazed to watch badminton players from four of the top eight teams on the planet repeatedly serve into the net or knock shots well out of bounds.

That year, one of the two teams of women from China (Tian Qing and Zhao Yunlei) was clearly dominant. However, they had lost an earlier match in the group play matches and were, unusually, ranked second as they entered the knockout rounds. That meant that other higher qualifiers would have to play them prior to the finals. While the top Chinese team would likely make a comeback and win the gold, the others would probably lose early on, destroying their chance at silver or bronze medals.

A badminton official at the London Games of 2012 warns players from Indonesia and South Korea against playing to lose.

Two teams from South Korea, a second team from China, and one from Indonesia found themselves in the awkward position of having their coaches order them to lose. Shocked, the officials sternly warned each team against throwing points. None of the four teams gave their best effort, and all four teams were eventually disqualified from the Games.

In 2012 the team of Tian/Zhao did win the gold medal, while Japan and Russia took the silver and bronze medals, respectively. Since the 2012 debacle, the rules have been changed to allow for a random draw going into the knockout rounds, thereby eliminating a team's incentive to lose earlier in the tournament.

• STAT BOX •

Unfair Play

Below are a few Olympians who have been caught cheating—not counting performance-enhancing drug use.

- Ortrun Enderlein (luge, 1968, German Democratic Republic) heated the rails on her sleds to ride faster.
- Boris Onischenko (modern pentathlon, 1976, U.S.S.R.) rigged his fencing épée to register hits that never happened.
- Madeline de Jesus (track & field, 1984, Puerto Rico) allowed her twin sister to run in her place.
- Dong Fangxiao (gymnastics, 2000, China) lied about her age.
- Bertil Sandstrom (equestrian, 1932, Sweden) used clicking noises to encourage his horse, against dressage rules.
- In 1960 the Tunisian modern pentathlon team sent up the same fencer hidden behind his mask, in the place of multiple other fencers.

Q: Some nations have added the Olympic rings to their national flags in order to participate in the Olympic Opening Ceremony. Which flags have been so altered?

Every Olympic year from 1984 to 2018, at least one country has carried a flag decorated with the Olympic rings.

A: German flag and Chinese Taipei flag

Luger Chih-Hunh carries the Chinese Taipei Olympic flag into the Vancouver 2010 Opening Ceremony; the flag was designed in 1984 solely for Olympic use.

When Germany was divided into the German Democratic Republic (East Germany) and the Federal Republic of Germany (West Germany) at the end of World War II, their sporting programs were also separated. However, athletes from both countries competed as a unified Germany in the 1956, 1960, and 1964 Games. Beginning in 1960, the teams marched under the old German tricolor flag, which had the Olympic rings superimposed in the center to show their unity in Olympic sport. However, in the 1968 Olympic Winter Games, the two Germanys entered separate teams under separate national flags, but each flag still bore the Olympic rings. Only after the 1989 reunification of Germany did the country return to one national flag, starting with the 1992 Games in Barcelona.

In 1949 the Communist-controlled People's Republic of China (PRC) forced the Republic of China (ROC) to retreat to the island of Taiwan. The PRC then participated in the 1952 Games, and the ROC boycotted them in protest. From 1956 to 1972 the PRC withdrew from the Olympic Games. In the late 1970s the PRC wanted to rejoin the Olympic movement and pressured the International Olympic Committee to deny the ROC the right to use the name and flag of China. Therefore, ever since the 1984 Olympic Winter Games, ROC athletes have marched under a specially designed Chinese Taipei Olympic flag featuring the stylized sun from the national flag and the Olympic rings.

• STAT BOX •

A Flag for All Athletes

Various athletes have marched under the Olympic flag instead of their national flag.

- **1992:** Athletes from the former nation of Yugoslavia and from the Republic of Macedonia had no national Olympic committees so they marched as Independent Olympic Participants.
- **2000, 2012, 2014, and 2016:** Various athletes from East Timor, South Sudan, India, and other nations competed as refugees or Independent Olympians when their countries had no recognized Olympic committees.
- **2018:** At the Olympic Winter Games in PyeongChang, South Korea, North and South Korean athletes marched together under a flag specially designed for the Olympic Games—the silhouette of both countries in blue against a white background, but without rings. The athletes competed together on the women's ice hockey team, and an athlete from each country held the flagpole.

Q: Other than the bullets used for shooting events, what is the fastest moving object in Olympic competition?

Hint:

It moves very quickly, but only for a short period of time.

A: Badminton shuttlecock

China's Lin Dan gently taps the shuttlecock over the net to Korea's Lee Hyun Il (not pictured) in a semifinal match at the 2012 Olympic Games in London; other times, he sent it speeding at approximately 200 miles an hour (322 km/h).

The shuttlecock (also called a birdie or shuttle) is the high-drag projectile hit back and forth across the net in the game of badminton. The shuttle used in the Olympic Games weighs less than two ounces (57 g) and is made of cork and goose feathers. Recreational shuttles are often made of more durable plastic. The shuttle can come off the racket at more than 200 miles an hour (322 km/h) when struck by an elite player.

The shuttle design forces the feathers to collapse at first and then to open quickly so the shuttle slows down precipitously. In an amazing display of focus, coordination, quickness, and endurance, the gold-medal point at the 2012 Olympic Games went 44 volleys across the net before Lin Dan (China) defeated Lee Chong Wei (Malaysia) with a score of 21–19 in the third game of a best-of-three series.

Badminton is one of the rare sports in which the United States has never earned an Olympic medal. Other summer sports in which Team USA has not medaled are rhythmic gymnastics, trampoline, table tennis, and team handball. New sports added to the 2021 Tokyo Olympic Games include karate, surfing, sport climbing, and skateboarding.

• STAT BOX •

Olympic Speed

Both athletes and objects aim for top speed in the Olympic Games.

- Arrow's flight: 150 mph (241 km/h)
- Tennis ball serve: approx. 129 mph (208 km/h)
- Clay pigeon flight: 41 mph (66 km/h)
- Platform dive: 35 mph (56 km/h)
- Gold-medal sprinter Usain Bolt (2008, 2012, 2016) at his fastest: 27.8 mph (44.7 km/h)

Q: Which U.S. Olympic champion is credited with sinking the longest golf putt ever recorded on video in a professional or pro-am event?

Although golf is now an Olympic sport, it was not when this golfer made his long putt.

A: Michael Phelps

After his remarkable success at the 2008 Olympic Games in Beijing (where he set the single Games record of eight gold medals), Phelps received regular invitations to participate in celebrity golf tournaments and pro-am events.

The remarkable putt happened on October 5, 2012, just weeks after he won six medals in London in his fourth Olympic Games. The athlete, known for his incredible swimming results in the pool (28 Olympic medals between 2000 and 2016), accomplished an amazing feat on land. On the sixth hole of the Old Course in St. Andrews, Scotland, the 26-handicap golfer reached the edge of the par-4 green on a long drive but was still almost 48.7 meters (160 ft) away from the flag. The television announcers had enough time to discuss his various swimming successes while the ball made its 17-second journey from the face of his putter down a slow incline before finally dropping into the cup.

Olympic champion swimmer Michael Phelps in a golf tournament at The Old Course in St. Andrews, Scotland

Phelps gave much of the credit to Hank Haney, one of golf-legend Tiger Woods's previous coaches. Haney had helped the swimmer with his golf game earlier that year, a process documented in eight episodes of the reality series *The Haney Project,* which aired on the Golf Channel in fall 2013.

I'm hugely proud to have been part of an Olympics, to be able to call myself an Olympian.

—Matt Kuchar
(golf, 2016, 1 bronze medal, PGA's top money winner in 2010)

Olympic Golf

Golf was first included on the 1900 and 1904 Olympic programs. In 1908 George Lyon from Canada traveled to London to defend his 1904 title, but an internal dispute canceled the event. Organizers offered Lyon, as the only competitor, the gold medal. He gracefully refused to accept it because he had not won it through proper competition.

Charles Edward Sands of the United States won the gold medal for golf at the 1900 Olympic Games in Paris.

Q: In what Olympic team sport was the United States guaranteed to win a gold medal before the championship final even began?

Hint:

It actually happened twice!

A: Beach volleyball

Two U.S. women's beach volleyball teams competed for gold in London in 2012: Kerri Walsh Jennings, center, and Misty May-Treanor (right) won.

Beach volleyball (along with badminton) is the rare team sport where each country may qualify more than one team into the Olympic tournament. In 1996 and in 2012, two U.S. teams faced each other in the championship match—guaranteeing a U.S. win.

Beach volleyball made its Olympic debut in 1996 at the Centennial Olympic Games in Atlanta, and because the United States was hosting those Games, three American teams were allowed to compete. Two of those teams advanced to the final, where Karch Kiraly and Kent Steffes defeated Mike Dodd and Mike Whitmarsh to win the gold in two straight games. The third U.S. team of Carl Henkel and Sinjin Smith finished in fifth place. Brazil won both gold and silver in the women's event that year.

At the 2012 Games in London, two American teams again advanced to the gold-medal match, where Misty May-Treanor and Kerri Walsh Jennings defeated Jennifer Kessy and April Ross in two games. This was May-Treanor and Walsh Jennings's third consecutive Olympic title.

• STAT BOX •

They're Golden

Several U.S. teams have won consecutive Olympic titles:

- **Men's swimming medley relay (1984-2016, nine titles)**
- **Men's basketball (1936-1968, seven titles)**
- **Women's basketball (1996-2016, six titles)**
- **Women's rowing eights: (2008-2016, three titles)**

One national team has won eight consecutive Olympic titles:

- **South Korea women's archery team (1988-2016, eight titles)**

A Winner Inside and Out

Karch Kiraly led the U.S. team to volleyball gold in 1984 and 1988. In 1996 he and his partner Kent Steffes won the first ever Olympic beach volleyball title and he is the only person to win Olympic medals both indoors and out. In 2009 he became the first member of a sport team to be inducted into the U.S. Olympic Hall of Fame as an individual.

U.S. men's beach volleyball champion Karch Kiraly at the Centennial Olympic Games

Q: Who was the first and, as of 2020, the only athlete to receive an Olympic medal while wearing another Olympic medal?

Hint:

This athlete received the two medals just minutes apart.

A: Steve Langton

Driver Steve Holcomb and brakeman Steve Langton were integral to the American two-man and four-man bobsled teams at the 2014 Olympic Winter Games in Sochi, Russia. In both events, the Americans finished third, receiving their bronze medals behind the gold-medal-winning performances of the Russian driver, Aleksander Zunkov, and his brakeman, Aleksei Voyevoda. Switzerland won silver in the two-man event, and Latvia came in second in the four-man event. In 2019 the International Olympic Committee (IOC) announced that both gold medals would be revoked because the Russians had tested positive in a re-test of their 2014 Olympic samples for performance-enhancing drug (PED) use. The runner-up teams from Switzerland and Latvia would receive the gold medals; and the Americans would be upgraded to silver medals for each event.

U.S. bobsledder Steven Langton is awarded a silver medal in 2019, upgraded from the bronze he received in 2014.

Traditionally, an IOC member presents the medals, and it was at the annual Team USA Awards in 2019 in Los Angeles when American IOC members Anita DeFrantz and Kikkan Randall made the presentations. Sadly, Holcomb had passed away in 2017, but Langton, along with Holcomb's family, was happy to receive the two-man silver medal. Langton then waited on stage for his four-man teammates, Chris Vogt and Curt Tomasevicz, to join him to receive the four-man silver medals. Langton had not removed his two-man award, and when the four-man medal was draped around his neck, a loud clang was heard as the second medal bounced against the first.

The sound informed the audience that this was a unique moment in Olympic history: An Olympic medal was being presented to an athlete already wearing one. For this to happen again, someone must finish in one of the top four places in two Olympic events, while someone finishing ahead of them in both events must have their medals revoked, and the two medal presentations must occur on the same day and at the same place.

• STAT BOX •

Performance-Enhancing Drugs (PEDs)

Several U.S. Olympic medalists have lost their Olympic medals after testing positive for banned substances, including the following:

- Rick DeMont, 1972, swimming
- Marion Jones, 2000, track & field
- Antonio Pettigrew and Jerome Young, 2000, track & field
- Lance Armstrong, 2000, cycling
- Tyler Hamilton, 2004, cycling
- Tyson Gay, 2012, track & field

Q: What U.S. city was awarded the rights to host an Olympic Games and later voluntarily gave them back to the International Olympic Committee (IOC) to award to another city?

Hint:

The IOC then awarded those Games to a city that had not bid for them, although that city had hosted the Games once before.

A: Denver, Colorado, returned the 1976 Olympic Winter Games, which were eventually awarded to veteran host Innsbruck, Austria.

Uh-Oh!

In summer 1972 Denver residents celebrated the naming of their city to host the 1976 Olympic Winter Games. Later, Denver turned down the honor.

On May 12, 1970, Denver was selected over Sion (Switzerland), Tampere (Finland), and Vancouver/Garibaldi (Canada) for the right to host the 1976 Olympic Winter Games.

On November 7, 1972, the people of Colorado voted in a statewide referendum to not be responsible for the cost of hosting the Games. A week later, the organizing committee returned the Games to the IOC.

Salt Lake City, Utah, offered to host the Games but, now wary of American cities, the IOC refused. Whistler, Canada, was then offered the Games, but the city declined after a change in government following recent elections. None of the other bidding cities were given the honor, and, on February 5, 1973, the IOC announced that Innsbruck, Austria, the host of the 1964 Olympic Winter Games, would be the new home of the 1976 Olympic Games, in part because it had many Olympic venues still in operation.

• STAT BOX •

Winter Hosts

These cities have hosted the Olympic Winter Games multiple times:

- **Innsbruck, Austria (1964, 1976)**
- **St. Moritz, Switzerland (1928, 1948)**
- **Lake Placid, New York (1932, 1980)**
- **Cortina d'Ampezzo, Italy (1956, and will in 2026)**

Aiming High

No city in the world has attempted to host the Olympic Games as often as Los Angeles. Before bidding was formalized, unofficial inquiries were submitted for the Games of 1924, 1928, and 1932. The Southern California Committee for the Olympic Games (SCCOG) bid for the city in 1948, 1952, and 1956, and the city tried again for the 1960, 1964, 1968, 1972, 1976, 1980, 1984, 2012, 2016, 2024, and 2028 Games. Hosting rights have been theirs three times: for the 1932, 1984, and the forthcoming 2028 Olympic Games.

Los Angeles Memorial Coliseum during the 1932 Olympic Games Opening Ceremony; also the site for the 1984 and 2028 Olympic Games

Q: What Olympic sport was the first to use video replay?

Hint: It was used when an official in an individual event was unsure of their decision.

A: Alpine skiing

The 1960 Olympic Winter Games in Squaw Valley, California, were the first Games to be shown on American television. CBS paid $50,000 for the right to broadcast them, not including the cost of setting up their cameras, talent, and facilities.

On the alpine slopes of KT-22 in Squaw Valley, in the men's slalom competition, officials were uncertain if one athlete had skied around the correct side of a gate. They asked Tony Verna, a member of the CBS production staff, to replay taped video footage to confirm the correct ruling. This gave Verna the idea to develop the Instant Replay system, which he introduced to the viewing audience during a televised football game three years later.

Verna went on to become a director and producer for many major live events, including the Kentucky Derby, Super Bowl, Goodwill Games, Olympic Games, and Live Aid concerts.

French skier François Bonlieu did not medal at the 1960 Olympic Winter Games in Squaw Valley, California, but won gold in Innsbruck, Austria, in 1964.

• STAT BOX •

Broadcasting Boon

The IOC has seen Olympic broadcasting rights revenues (below in U.S. dollars) soar through the years.

- 1960, Rome: $1.2 million
- 1968, Mexico City: $9.8 million
- 1976, Montreal: $35 million
- 1984, Los Angeles: $287 million
- 1992, Barcelona: $636 million
- 2000, Sydney: $1.332 billion
- 2008, Beijing: $1.739 billion
- 2016, Rio de Janeiro: $2.868 billion

Global Coverage

In 2001 the IOC established the Olympic Broadcasting Services (OBS) to provide a host broadcast of consistent radio and television sound and pictures of the Games to all rights-paying countries. In 2016 the OBS (left) used more than 7,200 personnel and 1,000 cameras to provide 350,000 hours of "world feed" coverage of the 28 sports in Rio de Janeiro.

Q: Throughout Olympic history, various athletes have competed in multiple Games and also marched under various flags. One athlete marched under four different flags without ever changing citizenship. What are the four flags?

Hint:

In one instance, this athlete's country was not allowed to send a team to the Olympic Games.

A: Yugoslavia, Independent Olympic Participants, Federal Republic of Yugoslavia (Serbia and Montenegro), and Serbia

In 2008 the Serbian delegation enters the Opening Ceremony of the Olympic Games in Beijing behind flag bearer and shooting champion Jasna Šekarić.

Jasna Šekarić was born in Belgrade, in then Yugoslavia, in 1965. Twenty-three years later, she was a member of the Yugoslavian shooting team at the 1988 Olympic Games in Seoul, South Korea, where she won gold in the 10-meter air pistol competition and a bronze medal in the 25-meter event. Four years later, her country was placed under UN sanctions and she tried to defend her title as an Independent Olympic Participant. She won a silver medal that year and marched under the Olympic flag along with 50 other athletes from Serbia, Montenegro, and Macedonia.

From 1996 to 2004 Serbia and Montenegro had jointly split from the Yugoslav Republic, and Šekarić marched under her third flag, the Federal Republic of Yugoslavia. By the 2008 Games in Beijing, Serbia had become its own nation, and she was chosen to carry the Serbian flag into the Opening Ceremony. At the 2012 Games in London, Šekarić competed in her seventh Olympic Games, once again under the Serbian flag.

I can help you with that. It's in my suitcase.

—Hal "Harry" Prieste (diving, 1920, 1 bronze medal), when asked in 1997 about the whereabouts of the original Olympic flag. He returned it to the IOC in 2000.

Under Many Flags

One other athlete has marched under four flags, but he changed citizenship to do so. Table tennis player Ilija Lupulesku competed in five Olympic Games. He represented Yugoslavia in 1988 and was an Independent Olympic Participant in 1992. He played for the Federal Republic of Yugoslavia (Serbia and Montenegro) in 1996 and 2000. In 2002 he became an American citizen, and represented the United States in Athens in 2004.

Playing table tennis for the United States, Ilija Lupulesku competes at the 2004 Olympic Games in Athens.

Q: Besides the United States, one other country received a standing ovation as its athletes came through the tunnel and into the Los Angeles Memorial Coliseum during the Opening Ceremony at the 1984 Olympic Games. Which country was it, and why were they so beloved?

Hint: The ovation was due to the country's political courage.

A: Romania

On May 8, 1984, the Soviet Union announced its boycott against the 1984 Olympic Games in Los Angeles, citing security concerns about anti-Soviet violence and the commercialization of the Games. However, many felt that this was a political move in response to the 66-country boycott of the 1980 Olympic Games in Moscow, led by the United States. In 1984 the Soviet Union held remarkable sway over many Eastern-bloc countries, including East Germany, Hungary, Poland, and Bulgaria. By the end of May, 13 countries had joined its boycott, including most Eastern-bloc nations, as well as Vietnam, North Korea, and Cuba.

• STAT BOX •

Dedicated Olympic Nations

From 1900 to 2020 these nations have participated in every Olympic Summer or Winter Games:

Summer:
Australia, France, Great Britain, Greece, and Switzerland

Winter:
Austria, Canada, Finland, France, Great Britain, Hungary, Italy, Norway, Poland, Sweden, Switzerland, and the United States

Romania's Doina Melinte crosses the finish line to win gold in the 800-meter event at the 1984 Games in Los Angeles.

Unexpectedly, Romanian dictator Nicolae Ceaușescu defied the Soviet Union's call to join the boycott, and his nation became the only Eastern-bloc nation to participate in the 1984 Olympic Games. When the Romanian athletes entered the coliseum, the crowd rose in appreciation of their political courage. The country's 124 athletes competed in 86 events in 13 sports, earning 57 medals—including more gold medals (20) than any country except the United States.

First Perfect 10s

At the 1976 Games in Montreal, 14-year-old Romanian gymnast Nadia Comaneci became an American favorite because of her perfect routines on the balance beam and uneven bars. She earned the first perfect 10.0 awarded in Olympic gymnastics history, eventually earning seven perfect scores in Montreal. Her infectious smile was also a welcome counterpoint to the stern faces of former Soviet winners. At the 1980 Games in Moscow, she earned an additional two gold and two silver medals. By 1984 Comaneci had retired from competition, but she came to Los Angeles at the request of the Games' organizers. Seated in a VIP box in the coliseum, she welcomed her country's delegation into the Opening Ceremony.

Romanian gymnast Nadia Comaneci on the balance beam at the 1976 Games in Montreal

Q: In what sport and year did an American Olympic champion hear the U.S. national anthem sung a cappella by her countrymen at the event?

Hint:

The sport and year make sense when considering the host country and city.

A: Taekwondo, 1988 Olympic Games, Seoul

In many Olympic Games, the host country was allowed to introduce new sports by adding demonstration or exhibition events. In 1988 the organizers in South Korea decided to place the national sport of taekwondo (a martial arts contest with roundhouse kicks and jabs) on the program, with both men's and women's events. Because it was not an official sport, the seats—in a large venue with plenty of seating—were sold at lower prices than the higher-profile events. U.S. military forces stationed at the nearby Demilitarized Zone (DMZ) were able to use their limited leave and resources to watch the Olympic Games in person.

Arlene Limas of the United States is awarded the victory in the gold medal bout in the demonstration sport of taekwondo at the 1988 Olympic Games in Seoul.

In the women's competition, the American welterweight entry, Arlene Limas, a 22-year-old honors student of Mexican and Polish descent, advanced through the early rounds to face South Korea's favorite, Kim Ji-Sook, in the final. Limas defeated her opponent and became the first gold medalist for the United States at the 1988 Olympic Games in Seoul.

Each venue had cassette tapes so any winner could hear their country's anthem after receiving their medallion. When it came time to play "The Star Spangled Banner" for Limas, the tape broke and static filled the venue. The volume was quickly turned down.

Then members of Limas's family began to sing. Soon, two U.S.

After receiving her gold medal, Arlene Limas gives a thumbs-up to her family and friends who sang the U.S. national anthem when the recording failed.

I felt the full spectrum of emotion, from confusion and disappointment when the flags flew in silence, to pride and joy when my family, friends, and U.S. military began singing out loud. It was amazing.

—Arlene Limas (taekwondo, 1988, 1 gold medal)

servicemen near the front of the arena were on their feet and proudly belting out the next line of the anthem. More of the soldiers joined in, and eventually every American present in the stands was singing out loud for the newest champion. At last, Limas joined in the singing of what may be the most emotional rendering of a national anthem in Olympic history.

Golden Slam

At the 2012 Olympic Games in London, in the world-famous Wimbledon tennis stadium, American Serena Williams won the singles title gold medal, and with her sister, Venus, the doubles gold. In so doing, she became the only player in history to earn a "Career Golden Slam" in both singles and doubles—winning Olympic gold and titles in all four tennis Grand Slam events. Ironically, as the U.S. national anthem played after one of her medal presentations, a gust of wind blew the American flag off its mounting, and the flag dropped unceremoniously to the ground. In response, Williams just smiled.

At the London Games in 2012, tennis champion Serena Williams (center on the medal podium) watches a falling American flag.

Olympic Summer Sports as of 2021

The 2021 Olympic Games feature 33 sports (50 disciplines) and 339 events.

- Aquatics
  - Artistic swimming
  - Diving
  - Swimming
  - Water polo
- Archery
- Athletics (track & field)
- Badminton
- Baseball
  - Baseball (new since 2008)
  - Softball (new since 2008)
- Basketball
  - Basketball
  - 3x3 Basketball (new)
- Boxing
- Canoe/Kayak
  - Slalom (whitewater)
  - Sprint (flatwater)
- Cycling
  - BMX freestyle (new)
  - BMX racing
  - Mountain biking
  - Road cycling
  - Track (velodrome) cycling
- Equestrian
  - Dressage
  - Eventing
  - Jumping
- Fencing
- Field hockey
- Football (soccer)
- Golf
- Gymnastics
  - Artistic
  - Rhythmic
  - Trampoline
- (Team) Handball
- Judo
- Karate
  - Kata (style) (new)
  - Kumite (combat) (new)
- Modern pentathlon
- Rowing
- Rugby sevens
- Sailing
- Shooting
- Skateboarding (new)
- Sport climbing (new)
- Surfing (new)
- Table tennis
- Taekwondo
- Tennis
- Triathlon
- Volleyball
  - Indoor
  - Beach
- Weightlifting
- Wrestling
  - Freestyle
  - Greco-Roman

Olympic Winter Sports as of 2021

The 2022 Olympic Winter Games feature seven sports (15 disciplines) and 109 events.

- Biathlon
- Bobsled
  - Bobsled
  - Skeleton
- Curling
- Ice hockey
- Luge
- Skating
  - Figure skating
  - Speed skating
  - Short track skating
- Skiing
  - Alpine skiing
  - Cross-country skiing
  - Freestyle Skiing
  - Nordic combined
  - Ski jumping
  - Snowboard

Paralympic Summer Sports as of 2021

The 2021 Paralympic Games feature 22 sports and 540 events.

- Archery
- Athletics (track & field)
- Badminton (new)
- Boccia
- Canoe
- Cycling
  - Road cycling
  - Track (velodrome) cycling
- Equestrian
- (Blind) Football (5-a-side)
- Goalball
- Judo
- Powerlifting
- Rowing
- Shooting
- Sitting volleyball
- Swimming
- Table tennis
- Taekwondo (new)
- Triathlon
- Wheelchair basketball
- Wheelchair fencing
- Wheelchair rugby
- Wheelchair tennis

Paralympic Winter Sports as of 2021

The 2022 Paralympic Winter Games feature 6 sports and 82 events.

- Alpine skiing
- Biathlon
- Cross-country skiing
- Sledge (ice) hockey
- Snowboard
- Wheelchair curling

About the Author

JOHN NABER was America's most decorated Olympian at the 1976 Games in Montreal, winning four gold and one silver medals in swimming. He won the James E. Sullivan Award as America's outstanding amateur athlete in 1977 and was inducted into the U.S. Olympic and Paralympic Hall of Fame in 1984. As of 2019, he's covered 10 Olympic and Paralympic Games for radio and television, and over 30 Olympic sports for various national networks, including ABC, NBC, CBS, TNT, and ESPN. He was twice elected president of the U.S. Olympians and Paralympians Association, and currently serves on the board of directors of the U.S. Olympic and Paralympic Committee, and as president of three Olympic-related nonprofit organizations: Olympians for Olympians Relief Fund, Koroibos Foundation, and Ready, Set, Gold! He is the author of *Awaken the Olympian Within* and *Eureka: How Innovation Changes the Olympic Games (and Everything Else)*. As a professional speaker, his programs cover topics including increased productivity, ethical behavior, and perpetual innovation. Naber lives with his wife, Carolyn, in Pasadena, California, where he has reported on more than 30 Rose Parades for the ABC television network.

Acknowledgments

The idea for this book came from Christopher Liedel, CEO of the new U.S. Olympic and Paralympic Museum in Colorado Springs, and without his support, this book would not exist. I also owe a huge debt of gratitude to my researcher of choice, Christina Snider, MMLIS, who superbly sourced all the facts in the book in real librarian fashion. Her meticulous attention to detail made my writing impossible to misunderstand, and each of her many suggestions made the book even better. Once the manuscript was finished, Barbara Brownell Grogan was invaluable in her editing, with help from photo editor Kristin Sladen, designer Carol Norton, and copyeditor Jane Sunderland. Kevin Mulroy brought his publishing expertise to the design, layout, and packaging of the final product. My thanks also go to the hundreds of Olympians and Paralympians who have shared their stories with me over the years.

About the Museum

A new cultural facility recognized by the International Olympic Committee, the United States Olympic and Paralympic Museum celebrates the stories of America's athletes. Spread over 60,000 square feet, the museum is located at the base of the Rocky Mountains in Colorado Springs, home of the United States Olympic Training Center. Featuring the latest audio and video technology, the museum's 13 interactive exhibits include the U.S. Olympic and Paralympic Hall of Fame. Visitors will witness the speed of a bobsled, race against the fastest runners ever, learn about technology in sport, and get up close to medals and torches from the world's greatest sporting spectacular. **www.usopm.org**

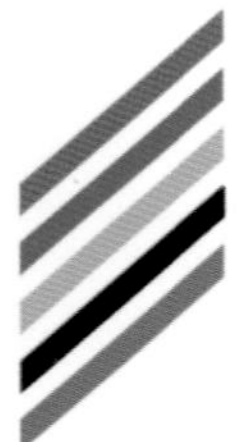

United States
Olympic
& Paralympic
Museum

14 Wallechinsky, David. (1991). *The complete book of the Olympics.* Little, Brown & Co.

16 Duguid, Sarah. (2012). Olga Fitoková, Czechoslovakia. FT Magazine, *Financial Times.*

18 Bijkerk, Anthony. (2001). *Rowing at the Games of the 2nd Olympiad.* Paris: 1900.

20 General Mills, Inc. (n.d.). General Mills: History of innovation: Wheaties, the breakfast of champions. *General Mills.* Retrieved from www.generalmills.com

22 Sports Reference, LLC. (n.d.). Gymnastics at the 1948 London Summer Games. *Sports Reference.* Retrieved from sports-reference.com

24 Historica Canada (2020). Canada at the Olympic Winter Games. *The Canadian Encyclopedia.* Retrieved from www.thecanadianencyclopedia.ca

26 International Olympic Committee. (2020). Paris 1900 Summer Olympics. Retrieved from www.olympic.org/paris-1900

28 International Olympic Committee. (2020). Olympic basketball's muddy beginnings. Retrieved from www.olympic.org

30 Library of Congress. (2018). Dates and locations of the modern Olympics. *Library of Congress.* Retrieved from www.loc.gov/rr/main/olympics/dates.html

32 International Olympic Committee. (2019). Hiroshi Hoketsu. Retrieved from www.olympic.org/hiroshi-hoketsu

34 New York City Police Department. (1950). Police athletes of the past: Patrick McDonald. *A Magazine for Policemen,* 21(10), 27, 31.

36 Watson, Stephanie. (2019). How Olympic torches work. *How Stuff Works.* Retrieved from https://entertainment.howstuffworks.com

38 International Olympic Academy. (2019). Coubertin Grove. *International Olympic Academy.* Retrieved from http://ioa.org.gr/coubertin-grove

40 Albanese, Joseph. (2019). The Kim Rhode story: Shotguns and family. *Range365.* Retrieved from www.range365.com

42 Guinness World Records, Limited. (2019). Oldest Olympic medalist. *Guinness World Records.* Retrieved from www.guinnessworldrecords.com

44 BBC Sports. (2012). Canada's Ian Millar to compete at record 10th games. *BBC.* Retrieved from https://www.bbc.com/sport/olympics/18742149

46 Askwith, Richard. (2016). Emil Zátopek: The man who changed running. *Runner's World.* Retrieved from www.runnersworld.com

48 Lozano, Juan A. (2003). Babe Zaharias was bigger than game. *Los Angeles Times.* Retrieved from www.latimes.com

50 L.A. Times Staff. (2007). Janice-Lee Romary, 79; fencer competed in 6 Olympic Games. *Los Angeles Times.* Retrieved from www.latimes.com

52 Banner, Larry. (2018). Biography: Pond, Charlie. *US Gymnastics Hall of Fame.* Retrieved from https://usghof.org/files/bio/c_pond/c_pond.html

54 Patzer, Nancy. (1999). The trial of Dr. James Snook. *Short North Gazette.* Retrieved from http://www.shortnorth.com/DrSnook.html

56 Jenkins, Sally. (2012). Why are Jim Thorpe's Olympic records still not recognized? *Smithsonian.* Retrieved from www.smithsonianmag.com

58 Calfas, Jennifer. (2018). Here's what happened at the first-ever Winter Olympics. *Time.* Retrieved from https://time.com/4993522/first-winter-olympics-1924-chamonix-france/

60 Bradshaw, Luke. (2016). Olympic heroes: Károly Takács and his wait for gold. *The Culture Trip.* Retrieved from https://theculturetrip.com

62 Lieberman, Stuart. (2016). Margaret Abbott aced Team USA's first women's Olympic gold medal and didn't know it. *Team USA.* Retrieved from https://www.teamusa.org

64 Thomas, Katie. (2010). Steinbrenner had quiet passion for the Olympics. *New York Times.* Retrieved from https://www.nytimes.com

66 Harkup, Kathryn. (2016). The cocktail of poison and brandy that led to Olympic gold. *The Guardian.* Retrieved from https://www.theguardian.com

68 Lusinski, Natalia. (2016). What is Jenny Thompson doing now? *Bustle.* Retrieved from https://www.bustle.com; Holter, Lauren. (2016). The way swimmer Natalie Coughlin is revving up for the Rio Olympics will astound you. *Bustle.* Retrieved from https://www.bustle.com; Shinn, Peggy. (2019). One for the ages: Hall of famer Dara Torres is swimming's oldest Olympic Medalist. *Team USA.* Retrieved from https://www.teamusa.org

72 Cox, Dwayne. (1984). Pole vault hero now Populist Party candidate. *United Press International.* Retrieved from https://www.upi.com/Archives/1984/08/18/Pole-vault-hero-now-Populist-Party-candidate/7788461649600; Andrews, Evan. (2016). Eight unusual presidential candidates. *History.* Retrieved from https://www.history.com/news/8-unusual-presidential-candidates

74 Turbow, Jason. (2012). George S. Patton (yes, that one) was a modern pentathlete. *Wired.* Retrieved from https://www.wired.com

76 Welch, Bob. (2018). *The wizard of Foz: Dick Fosbury's one-man high-jump revolution.* Skyhorse Publishing.

78 Mallenbaum, Carly. (2016). Why Ali's Hollywood star is on a wall (not the ground). *USA Today.* Retrieved from www.usatoday.com

80 International Olympic Committee. (n.d.). Speakers – Donna de Varona. Retrieved from https://www.olympic.org/olympism-in-action

82 Brooks, Janet Rae. (2000). Gender testing at Olympics abolished at last. *The Globe and Mail.* Retrieved from www.theglobeandmail.com

84 BBC News. (2011). Monaco's Prince Albert marries South African Charlene Wittstock. *BBC.* Retrieved from https://www.bbc.com/news/world-europe-13973248

86 Bauer, Patricia. (2017). Chariots of Fire. *Encyclopaedia Britannica.* Retrieved from https://www.britannica.com/topic/Chariots-of-Fire

88 Jacobs, Laura. (2014). Sonja Henie's ice age. *Vanity Fair.* Retrieved from www.vanityfair.com

90 International Swimming Hall of Fame. (n.d.). Johnny Weissmuller (USA). Retrieved from https://ishof.org; International Swimming Hall of Fame. (n.d.). Clarence "Buster" Crabbe (USA). Retrieved from https://ishof.org

92 Bomboy, Scott. (2016). The Supreme Court decision that saved Muhammad Ali's boxing career. *National Constitution Center.* Retrieved from https://constitutioncenter.org

94 Biography.com editors. (2014). Louis Zamperini biography. Retrieved from https://www.biography.com/military-figure/louis-zamperini

96 Tournament of Roses. (2019). Pasadena Tournament of Roses. Retrieved from https://tournamentofroses.com

100 Kavanaugh, Adam. (2016, June 14). A guide to track cycling. *BikeExchange.* Retrieved from BikeExchange.com

102 Swedish Olympic Committee. (1913). *The fifth Olympiad: The official report of the Olympic Games of Stockholm 1912.* Wahlström & Widstrand.

104 U.S. Olympic & Paralympic Committee. (n.d.). Carl Lewis. *Team USA.* Retrieved from www.teamusa.org

106 Eisenberg, Jeff. (2020). The only American to medal at the 1980 Olympics in Moscow. *Yahoo Sports.* Retrieved from https://sports.yahoo.com

108 Battaglia, Joe. (2016). Super Bowl champion reflects on bobsled beginnings. *Team USA.* Retrieved from www.teamusa.org

110 Vecsey, George. (2011). Indomitable Russell values one accolade above the rest. *New York Times.* Retrieved from www.nytimes.com

112 Welch, Bob. (2018). *The wizard of Foz: Dick Fosbury's one-man high-jump revolution.* Skyhorse Publishing.

114 Prosba, Zach. (2016). Top 10 U.S. summer Olympians of all time. *Hero Sports.* Retrieved from www.herosports.com

116 Pitoniak, Scott. (2008). Lochte swims to two medals 27 minutes apart. *Gannett News Service.* Retrieved from https://web.archive.org/web/20081211155305/http://www.usatoday.com/sports/olympics/beijing/swimming/2008-08-15-lochte_n.htm